NATIONAL ARCHAEOLOGICAL
MUSEUM ATHENS

NATIONAL ARCHAEOLOGICAL MUSEUM ATHENS

Newsweek / GREAT MUSEUMS OF THE WORLD

NEW YORK, N.Y.

**GREAT MUSEUMS
OF THE WORLD**

Editorial Director—Carlo Ludovico Ragghianti
American Editor—Henry A. La Farge

NATIONAL ARCHAEOLOGICAL MUSEUM ATHENS

Introduction by:
Barbara Philippaki

Critical texts by:
Licia Collobi Ragghianti

History of the Museum by:
Alan Leonard

Design:
Fiorenzo Giorgi

Published by
NEWSWEEK, INC.
& ARNOLDO MONDADORI EDITORE

2nd Printing 1980

INTRODUCTION

Barbara Philippaki
Director, National Archaeological Museum of Athens

Museum is a Greek word, and the first center of intellectual activity known to us by that name was the Museum connected with the famous Library in the Palace of the Ptolemies, in the great Hellenistic city of Alexandria, founded by Alexander the Great in 332 B.C. But already a century earlier, in the Athens of Pericles, the instinct to preserve works of art was evident in a collection of paintings which had been gathered together on the north side of the Propyleum of the Acropolis, in a large hall called the Pinakothiki (picture gallery).

Although the Greeks lived for centuries under foreign rule, the memory of their glorious past never left them, and they retained a reverence for the splendid monuments of their ancestral inheritance. But this was not enough to prevent the ravages of time and human ignorance.

At the beginning of the nineteenth century there were foreigners living in Athens who began to be interested in the preservation of antiquities, and had collections of ancient art, mostly sculptures and numismatics. The best known were those of the French consul, Louis Fauvel and the British historian George Finlay. But with the rise of the national consciousness the first significant attempt of the still subjugated Greeks to found a museum was in 1813, when the Philomouson (Lovers of the Muses) organized efforts to preserve ancient monuments and collect antiquities, "so that lovers of these things could view them." In 1824 the Philomouson tried in vain to have such antiquities as were already collected placed in the Erechtheum. In these dramatic attempts, which persisted throughout the struggle for liberation, many intellectuals participated, the most prominent of whom was the Greek patriot Adamantios Koraes.

One significant attempt to protect the country's antiquities—now with legal action—was the law prohibiting the export of ancient works of art, which was promulgated by the Third National Assembly, elected at Epidauros.

In March 1829, with the nation finally free and under the enlightened leadership of Greece's first governor, Ioannes Kapodistrias, a National Museum was founded on the island of Aegina, then the provisional capital of the new state. The antiquities of all the provinces were collected there, either through purchase from their owners—many of whom were peasants who had unearthed them while cultivating their land—or as gifts "from patriotic citizens and lovers of beauty."

But when on September 28, 1834, the capital of the nation moved to Athens, the Aegina Museum became a regional museum, and most of its holdings were transferred to the Central Archaeological Museum in Athens, which had already been founded. The Aegina Museum retained only those antiquities which had been found on the island itself and had not been exported, such as the sculptures of the Temple of Aphaea. In Athens, the Central Archaeological Museum was first housed in the Theseion, one of the best preserved ancient temples, identified today as the Temple of Hephaistos. Except for the antiquities found in Athens and Piraeus, works of art from all parts of the country were now brought to the Central Museum. Additional space was soon required, and the fifth-century church of Megalis Panayia together with the Stoa of Hadrian were opened for this use.

In 1837, the Athenian Archaeological Committee was founded in an official ceremony which took place in the sacred precincts of the Parthenon, with the express purpose of collecting antiquities, preserving monuments and regulating excavations. Under its direction, all objects either from its excavations or acquired by purchase were housed in the Varvakeion Lyceum and the Metsove Polytechnic School, both Neoclassic buildings, the first of which was built in 1857, and the second in 1862.

By the early 1860s the great mass of ancient art collected now created an imperative need to found a large museum, capable of adequately housing all these objects under one roof. This need was provided for by a generous gift from Demetrios Bernardakis, and the building of a new museum was launched, on a plot of land donated by Elena Tositsa. The original design for the building was drawn by the German architect Ludwig Lange, and by 1885 the west, north and south wings of a quadrangle around a central court were built. Lange's plan was then modified by another German architect, Ernst Ziller, under whose designs the east wing, the central hall, and the colonnade of the stoa were built. The new museum, with its imposing Neoclassic rhythm, was a one-story structure with a magnificent entrance, a large garden in front, and trees on the other three sides.

The building was only completed in 1889, but objects began being transferred to it as early as 1874. Thus slowly all the antiquities which up to that time had been stored in the Theseion, the Megalis Panayia church, the "Tower of the Winds," the "Parliament," the Varvakeion and the Polytechnic School were collected in one place. Also brought over were the gravestones in sculptural relief from the renowned ancient cemetery of the Kerameikos, the bas-reliefs from the excavations on the south slope of the Acropolis, and epigraphs from the same Acropolis. But the finest sculptures and pottery from the provinces were also gathered at the new museum, from such provinces as Delos, Melos, Naxos, Keros, Amorgos, Syros and other islands of the Cyclades; others were collected from Tanagra, Thespis, Thebes, Larissa, Tegea, Argos—all towns of the mainland—as well as sculptures from the excavations in the sanctuary of Asklepios in Epidauros. Along with these were many bronzes from Olympia and from the Acropolis. In addition were the bas-reliefs dedicated to the protectress of the Athenians, which had come to light in the great excavations of the Acropolis.

Initially called the Central Archaeological Museum, the name was changed in April 1888 to the National Archaeological Museum, by which it has been known ever since. But in the course of one generation from its dedication, the building was no longer large enough to put under one roof the mass of antiquities which had been pouring into it daily from the great excavations of the fifty years from 1876 to 1925, and it was then decided to extend it to the east. These endeavors lasted until 1939. The eastern side of the Museum is now two-storied, but without this being perceptible from the western facade. Many large rooms were added for workshops, and additional parts to serve as storerooms and basements.

The outbreak of World War II and the dramatic days which followed for the country not only put a stop to the development of new space, but created the urgent necessity of immediately hiding all the museum's treasures, safely stored for all contingencies. After the war, the National Archaeological Museum had the good fortune to come under the enlightened direction of Christos and Semni Karouzos. With the keen awareness of the great responsibilities which only deep knowledge can dictate, and backed by a staff of excellent technicians, this husband-and-wife team gave the best part of themselves for many years. They provided an exemplary model of museum administration, from which valuable lessons have been drawn both for postwar Greek exhibitions and for foreign museums.

However, even now the display of all the museum's holdings could not be completed, due to lack of space. In the storerooms of the museum a mass of objects awaited their turn to be placed on view. It is necessary only to mention the black-figure (*melanvaphy*) and Hellenic vases; the large collection of clay idols (terracottas), which occupies an important place in the well-known Misthou Collection; pieces of gold and jewelry from every part of Greece, especially valuable because they originate from known, well-dated excavations; the interesting Alexandrian pieces from the Demetrios Collection; and even glassware, comprising small oil lamps, among which are examples from the Acropolis. The Museum also possesses an important collection of Cypriot antiquities and the well-known Empedocles Collection. The storerooms still abound in prehistoric pieces, besides sculptures and bronzes, representing works of interest mainly to specialists. In view of this the Museum is planning a new extension to acquire more space for all of these. One activity to which special attention is now being given is exhibitions aimed at education and a widening of public interest. Already two such shows, one titled the "Medical Exhibition," the other, "The Child in Antiquity," have been very successful.

The present permanent installations are divided into four outstanding categories: the sculptures (30 rooms); the vases (10 rooms); the prehistoric sculptures and objects (3 rooms); and the bronzes (4 rooms). In addition are the Karapanos Collection containing unusual bronzes from Dodona (p. 96) exhibited in special rooms, and the precious Helen

Stathatos Collection of gold jewelry, which has never before been placed on public exhibition. It is hoped that the Demetrios Collection—the only one of its kind in the land—will not long be delayed. It is still in preparation, along with the remaining section of the bronzes, and the sculptures of the Roman era, notable for its portraits.

A focus of interest which attracts the greatest number of visitors is the Mycenean Collection, which has no counterpart in the world, a nucleus containing the unparalleled discoveries from the tombs of the kings in the Acropolis of the "golden" Myceneans, brought to light by the genius of Heinrich Schliemann. Among these can also be seen other remarkable objects of the Mycenean civilization, such as the gold cups from Vapheio (p. 43), the gold signet rings from Tiryns (p. 37), the unique ivory group of *Two Goddesses and a Divine Child* (p.53). Most astonishing is the impression of wealth and variety given by the exhibits in this room, exemplifying the virtuosity and depth of creativity which the Myceneans reached in working precious metals, ivory, and semiprecious stones, and their daring conception of the themes depicted.

In contrast, the relief decorations on the stone pillars which adorned the Mycenean tombs seem very inferior. Yet these are the earliest epitaph monuments that we have. In the same room are displayed some of the clay tablets from Pylos and Mycenae which show inscriptions in the "Linear B" writing. One of these is P. 641, well known as having confirmed the theory of Michael Ventris that the language of the Myceneans was Greek, and thus that they were Greeks.

Hardly less remarkable is the room devoted to the cultures of the Cyclades. In these islands embraced by the Aegean, the extraordinary civilization which developed in the third millennium B.C. had an art which employed clay and the luminous Cycladic marbles for sculpture, producing miracles in both mediums. The superb Cycladic idols—the largest of which is 1.52 m. high—have a peculiar attraction to the modern eye in the effortless simplification of form drawn schematically, and vibrating with life. Along with these creations, the *Harpist* (p. 21) and the *Flutist,* two masterful works from Keros, give us a measure of the strength of the Cycladic artists. But the Cycladic artists distinguished themselves no less astonishingly in another field, namely painting, as manifested by the vases and frescoes of the second millennium from Melos and Thera (Santorini) (pp. 23–29). The recent excavations of Thera (2 rooms) have given us a "Prehistoric Pompeii," reclaimed from under the ashes and lava of a catastrophic volcanic eruption which annihilated a splendid civilization with a highly developed social structure. Notable among the masterpieces uncovered are the wall paintings, in which the art of fresco seems to be combined with tempera. Technique, themes, stylization, all show a close kinship to Crete. The same are observed in the vases. But the paintings of Thera have something of their own, an ethereal, bright, fresh quality unique to the Aegean. Both the fresco of *Spring* (p.

12

23) and the plant forms which prevail in pottery design are an expression of the sensitivity of the Aegean people and their harmonious association with the superb nature surrounding them.

In the third room of the Prehistoric section of the museum are displayed the findings of early excavations in Thessaly and the mainland of Greece, which established the foundations of prehistoric Greek archeology. The digs of recent years in Thessaly have greatly extended the chronology of the Neolithic period in this area; that is to say, there are now distinguished a protoceramic Neolithic period which is placed approximately in the seventh millennium, the early Neolithic in the sixth millennium, the middle Neolithic (Sesklo culture) in the fifth, and the later Neolithic (Dimini culture) in the fourth. Although the findings of the newer excavations, which are chronologically the oldest, are preserved in the Museum of Volos, marvelous representative examples are exhibited in the National Archaeological Museum, comprising clay idols and vases from the old excavations made by the great Greek archaeologist, Christos Tsountas, founder of the prehistory of Thessalonika.

Of enormous interest are the finds of the Neolithic and Bronze Age periods—the proto-Hellenic and the meso-Hellenic—from the mainland of Greece, and especially from Phthiotis, Locris, Boeotia, and Attica. The most astonishing work among these finds is the large clay male idol from Thessaly, unique in dimensions and conception, which may date from the third millennium B.C.

In the same room is also exhibited a part of the "Treasures of Troy," comprising a gift from Sophia Schliemann to the museum.

Especially notable are the museum's sculpture collections, which cover the whole historic range of ancient Greek sculpture. Most of the works originate from excavations and, but for a few exceptions, are original and from the best epochs of Greek art. It goes without saying that the masterpieces of the classic period have come down to us in copies of the Roman era.

The earliest statue in the museum's collections, barely 24 cm. high, is a nude female figure with a diadem on her head, something which identifies her as a deity (p. 64). Made of ivory, it is the earliest attempt of an Attic artist to carve a female figure (ca. 8th century B.C.) that has come down to us, of a type indicating the assimilation of Near Eastern art, probably Anatolian. In the Geometric period, to which this figure belongs, the ideal of the artist appears to have been to make clay, bronze or ivory works of small size.

Fully two hundred years later, another superb female figure, now a clothed statue, an offering of the Naxian Nikandris to Artemis in Delos, depicts either the goddess or

13

Nikandris herself. In the series of female statues recently donated to us by the Mesogeion of Attica, the excellent statue of a young woman called Phrasiclea was included, along with many other works. The statue of Phrasiclea was set over a tomb, because instead of a wedding the gods gave her death, as she herself tells us in the moving epigram at the base of the statue.

Where the sculpture collection is without equal is in the series of male nude statues of *kouroi* (young men). More than twenty-three kouroi, and more than thirteen kouroi heads—including the masterpiece from the Dipylon (p. 81)—offer inducement both to the special student and to the observant visitor to follow the evolution of the type within one century (from the end of the seventh to the end of the sixth century B.C.). In the simple conception of this type, strongly and schematically drawn, the essential requirements of anatomical detail are rendered with conventional forms for the most perfect embodiment of the physical and spiritual man, which constituted the great ideal of Greek civilization. Greek art embodied its gods in this same type, and human form was its most perfect creation in the epoch of its highest achievement, as in the god from Artemision (Poseidon or Zeus) (pp. 112–113). This god along with several other bronze masterpieces—including some heads—are part of a remarkable group of bronze originals which constitute one of the high points in the Museum's collections today. Added to these, the Museum excels in small bronzes, thanks to the rich and exceptional discoveries in the sanctuaries of the Athenian Acropolis, Olympia and Dodona.

Incomparable also is the collection of sculptural gravestones and votive reliefs. The philosophical confrontation of the mortal fate of man, and the serene resignation with which it is accepted opened up Greek art in the most ideal way to the carving of memorials for those who had departed, often very prematurely, in which the deceased is often represented accompanied by the tender solicitude of loved ones. Some one hundred and thirty-six of these grave reliefs and marble lekythoi fill all of five rooms of the museum, in addition to many more examples in the storage rooms.

The Museum's collection of vases is one of the richest in the world, and certain sections of it contain the most amazing examples of their kind. Nevertheless, as so often happens in even the largest collections, certain categories of vases are poorly represented. As regards Attic red-figure vases, the National Museum is lacking in examples by the greatest craftsmen and painters. This can be attributed to the fact that Solon, archon of Athens in 595 B.C., is said to have given great impetus to the export of vases by allowing admirers of Greek art outside the country, notably the Etruscans, to acquire masterpieces of this period, Attic in particular, and these vases followed them to their luxurious graves, where they have been found in large numbers. The modern interest in Greek vases began, properly speaking, in the seventeenth century, and from then on increased at an accelerating pace. The appreciation of their value continued to develop, with the result that today they are not only a source of pride in many museums, but also in great demand by private collectors in the most unlikely places in the world.

Except for a very few, the vases of the National Museum originate from excavations on Greek territory, from gifts, purchases and confiscation. First in terms of chronology of the outstanding sections of the collection are the Geometric (900–700 B.C.), represented by examples unparalleled in their harmony, unity, form and decoration. The large amphorae and kraters, up to 1.50 m. in height, are remarkable achievements of the Attic potters, made to stand over the graves of rich landowners as imposing monuments proclaiming wealth and power. From the seventh century the Attic workshops continue to astonish with their monument vases, now not only in their form, but also in their painted decoration. Representative examples of these amazing vases come from the well-known burial grounds of Vaphis and the great Athenian cemetery of the Kerameikos.

Another side of Greek art is the sensitivity and the restrained expression of pain and anguish before death, expressed in the white-ground lekythoi vases. Painted with line and color over very fine white glaze, they were destined only for funerary use. This kind of painting clearly derives from the great tradition of fresco painting, and also from panel paintings, unique examples of which have come down to us in small wooden votive tablets dating from the latter half of the sixth century which have been found in the cave of Pitsa, near Corinth (p. 93). Copies of these are displayed in the exhibition of vases, showing a relationship with small perfume vases from the Corinthian workshops, which are distinguished by a marvelous miniature rhythm, elegance and perfection of technique.

It is very instructive in the last room of vases to compare the production of the Corinthian and Viotikos workshops with the Attic vases from the last quarter of the fourth century, when the production of great painted vases came to an end. In order to appreciate the innate quality of Greek vases, it is important to remember that from a simple handcraft production for daily use, they attained peerless perfection as great works of art. Careful visual observation, together with some knowledge of Greek mythology and history cannot fail to bring us closer to perhaps the richest source for a knowledge and understanding of the ancient Greek world.

B. Philippaki

FOREWORD

The authors wish to remark that the texts which follow, rather than being mere compilations, are carefully considered observations containing essential information.

The interpretation of a succession of phenomena beginning with the Neolithic era, followed in orderly succession by the "Archaic," then by the so-called "mature" and finally by the "decadent" periods—in keeping with a widely expounded hypothesis of evolution—has been completely rejected. Instead, we have aimed at considering the various phenomena of Greek art occurring simultaneously or at different times with the idea of comprehending the intrinsic character and intellectual premises of each. From this point of view, the Archaeological Museum of Athens—which is an institution containing documents from the Aegean area and the Greek mainland—is particularly well adapted to demonstrate the plurality of independent civilizations, concepts of form, and cultures. These cannot be schematized according to logical sequences of development, in a preconceived system which fails to correspond to reality.

Since the Museum is notoriously lacking in works of some of the greatest and most famous artists, their achievements are recalled whenever it has been felt necessary or opportune to do so. In like manner, although perhaps more succinctly, reference is made from the start to certain intellectual and aesthetic bases affirming the instinct of creative expression which unite to form a millennial, vital tradition.

We hope that this anthological volume can contribute toward giving a fresh, untrammeled image of the course of Greek art, and perhaps also focus critical and analytical attention on works which are qualitatively outstanding in the absolute sense although they may at times have been less noticed and inadequately evaluated.

Licia and Carlo L. Ragghianti

**COMMENTARY TEXTS
AND PLATES**

NEOLITHIC HELLADIC CULTURE. *Mother and Child*
(Kourotrophos).   *p. 19*

This statuette of a woman holding a child, discovered in the excavations on the Acropolis of Sesklo in Thessaly, belongs to a late phase of Neolithic art, near the Bronze Age of Thessalian culture. Close attention to natural proportions is evident in the construction of the body; the legs are clearly differentiated from those of the supporting chair and rhythmically spaced but accurately individualized even in their analogous tubular forms, which are rigorously perpendicular, tapered, and full of life despite the relaxed position of the figure.

The polychrome decoration gives great liveliness to the statuette; the brown tones on the vivid yellow-pink background are a persistent characteristic of figurative representations of that epoch. These curvilinear segments serve to emphasize the volumetric mass of the limbs, functioning in exactly the same way as the decorative bands on the spherical surfaces of the contemporary burial urns and plates (some of which are in the Athens Museum). They also accent the anatomical description of details like the lap, synthesizing form in a vivid play of colors and lines for which the human figure is fundamentally the main vehicle. These continuous chromatic rings, moreover, serve to impose a rotating, expansive, spiralling movement on the body.

NEOLITHIC HELLADIC CULTURE
Mother and Child (Kourotrophos)
Ca. 4000 B.C.
Terracotta; height 6¼".
From Sesklo. (5937)

CYCLADIC CULTURE. *Concave Plate with Boat in a Sea of Waves.*   *p. 20*

This object was found on Syros, a flourishing island situated in the heart of the Aegean, at the center of the magnificent Stone and Bronze Age cultures known as "Cycladic" (5000–2000 B.C.). Owing to the wealth and variety of its mineral resources—obsidian, marble and, later, copper—even articles of daily use assume extraordinarily expressive and original forms. This is a famous example of a concave receptacle with a double-knobbed handle. It has been presumed that objects of this type had some ritual or possibly domestic application (they are popularly called "frying pans"). The shallow concave form has led to the supposition that it might have been filled with water and used as a mirror.

The object consists of a disk elongated at the lower end to form a handle. The running border is a flexibly curved double row of deep indentations on each side of a median ridge, creating a strongly accented chiaroscuro. Within the border, above the triangle at the base enclosing sprays of vegetation, a boat propelled by oars is depicted in a tumultuous sea of waves. The waves are agitated in a fantastic rhythm by a compressed network of rotating spirals with tails forming triangles, and if the plate is taken in hand and moved about, the effect of moving waves is incredibly heightened. This type of lyrical fantasy was evidently an innovation which, however, was to remain isolated, even though the dynamic motif of the repeated spiral was to be frequent in the art of the fourth, third and second millenniums (for example, in the Athens Museum, the bell-shaped vase from Dimini, no. 5927, and the stele from the Acropolis of Mycenae, p.40). The incessant rolling and glitter of the waves around the boat is effected by the geometry of the spirals, and creates a unique emotional vision vividly reflecting the seafaring life of the Cycladic people.

Works such as this reveal characteristics that were to remain constants of the poetic and artistic outlook of Greek civilization: the primary emotion and its sublimation are expressed not in contingent and perishable forms but in absolute, immutable conceptions.

CYCLADIC CULTURE
Concave Plate with Boat in a Sea of Waves
Ca. 2800–2200 B.C.
Dark Terracotta; diam. 11″.
From Syros. (4974)

CYCLADIC CULTURE. *Seated Harp Player.* p. 21
Found at Keros, this remarkable statuette is perhaps the most famous of the predominantly female figurations documenting the last flowering of the Cycladic civilization, between 2300 and 2100 B.C.

Comparing the many examples scattered in major world collections, it becomes evident that the treatment of the theme is not a question of repetitions or amplifications of a prototype but rather of compositional variations on the articulation of essentially stylistic elements, among which the triangle is the

P. 21
CYCLADIC CULTURE
Seated Harp Player
Ca. 2300–2100 B.C.
Marble; height 8¾″.
From Keros. (3908)

fundamental motif, associated with variously oriented cylindrical, conical and crescent-shaped forms.

The sculptor proceeded by aligning, counterbalancing, paralleling, angling, interpenetrating and inverting the triangular rhythms viewed both laterally and from above—with the head, nose, arms and legs indicating direction—as well as from the horizontal plane of the base. In other words, he employed a limpid binding stereometry in which the diffused light filtering through the translucent marble serves to heighten a contemplative meaning.

Pp. 22–23
ARTIST OF THERA
Mural Painting from the "Spring" Room, detail
Ca. 1500 B.C.
Fresco; height 98½".

ARTISTS OF THERA. *Mural Paintings: Spring (detail); Naval Battle; Antelopes; Fisherman.*   *pp. 23–29*

The discovery of the remains of a wealthy Minoan colony on the island of Thera—a flourishing center of civilized life—has vastly expanded our knowledge of ancient Hellenic cultures. According to Marinatos, the expert to whom we owe the most recent and exhaustive investigation of this important phenomenon, the island was suddenly submerged in the fifteenth century B.C. by a terrifying natural catastrophe—a cataclysm analogous to that which obliterated Pompeii fifteen centuries later. The thick layer of volcanic ashes that blanketed Thera was, however, instrumental in preserving buildings, paintings and objects existing at the moment of the appalling event.

The surviving mural decorations, which have been moved to the Athens Museum, are of great historical interest as documents of a culture that was contemporary with, and probably a link between, the civilization that flowered in Crete and that which arose in Argolis, in particular at Mycenae in the beginning of the seventeenth century B.C. The date now generally agreed upon for this art is approximately 1500 B.C., which coincides with the apex of Cretan civilization. Clearly in evidence are correspondences of subject matter, styles of headdress, techniques, and particular decorative components; although all these elements are elaborated with a resourcefulness and originality of vision and language, which have given rise to various hypotheses.

There can be no doubt that several easily distinguishable masters worked on these recently discovered mural paintings, although they are not all of an equally high qualitative level. The *Naval Battle,* (p. 24–25) with its tiny, miniature-like figures dwarfed by the vast panoramic setting might have been painted at a later date. The chronology and even the critical definition itself of the figurative phenomena of the so-called Minoan-Mycenaean era are still too uncertain—as are the dates of important events and historical migrations—to permit us to defend with conviction one or another of the many hypotheses that have been proposed.

As can be expected with prehistoric painting, these frescoes as they appear today in their restored condition are the result of patient reconstructions from surviving fragments which in some cases consist only of a small fraction of the whole. Yet the image which results is an intelligible, meticulous evocation of the original.

The noble rhythms of the proud *Fisherman* (p. 29)—heavily laden with his huge catch of fish, which enliven the space at either side with their scintillating color and the pointed outlines of their tails—have their counterpart in the wall of the *Spring* (p. 23) in the stupendous animation of the flowering tufts bursting

22

Above, and detail pp. 26 and 27
ARTIST OF THERA
Naval Battle
Ca. 1500 B.C.
Fresco; height 114″.

24

Below
ARTIST OF THERA
Mural Painting with River and Animals
Ca. 1500 B.C.

forth in wild disorder from craggy hillsides which—even in the alternation of four sober colors—expresses the unrestrained joyful magic rebirth of spring.

The long wall of the *Naval Battle* (pp. 24–27) is a painting of enormous vitality, overflowing with imagination and remarkable in the elegance and beauty of its formal language. It probably celebrates an epic event narrated in a heroic poem, and is thus of exceptional importance as a document of remote times, containing a precise record of places, customs and events depicted in a rapid stenographic idiom, and with rhythmic sensitivity of such high quality that it would be difficult to find its equal in the art of the time.

The bodies of the *Antelopes* (p. 28)—like those of the similarly painted but gravely damaged *Blue Monkeys*—are emphasized by the mobile tension of the drawing, achieved by the employment of sinuous ribbonlike outlines. This cloisonné-like effect recalls the fluid modeling of the antelopes in relief at Knossos, and of the rocky cliffs and the swallows in flight in the *Spring* room (p. 23)—confirming the substantial unity of these works.

ARTIST OF THERA
Antelopes
Ca. 1500 B.C.
Fresco; height 98½".

P. 29
ARTIST OF THERA
Fisherman
Ca. 1500 B.C.
Fresco; height 48½".

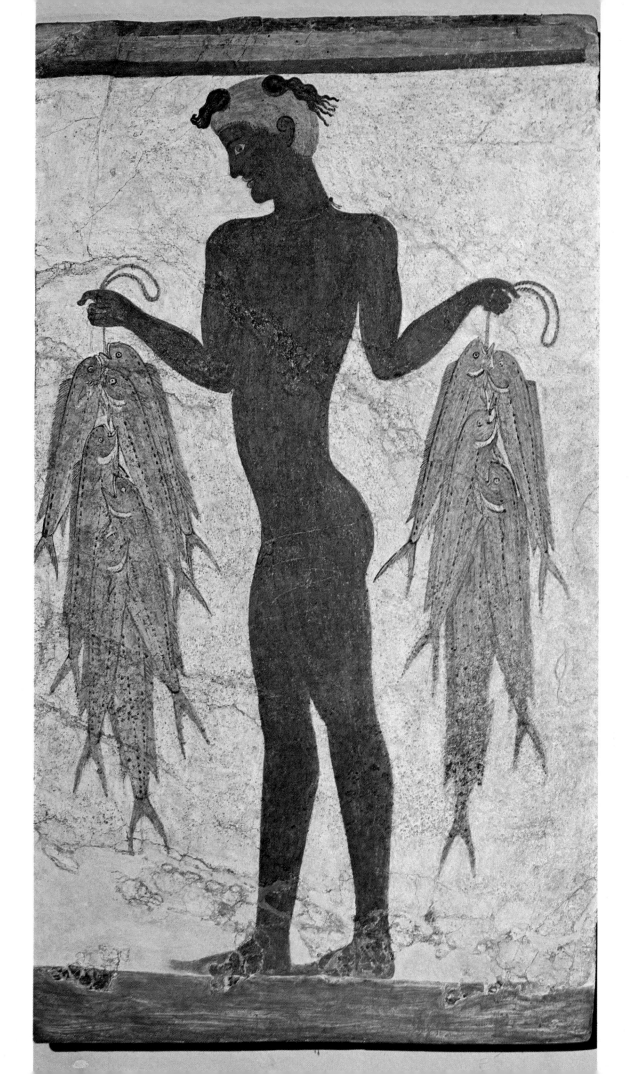

MINOAN(?) ARTIST
Rhyton, Head of a Bull
Sixteenth century B.C.
Gold leaf and silver; height 11¾″.
(384)

The solid gold rosette fixed with a stud on the forehead seems to epitomize the judicious distribution of gold leaf decoration on the ears, the nostrils and the large crescent-shaped (restored) horns. The missing eyes were perhaps of gold, niello or semiprecious stones.

Similar vessels in the form of lion or bull heads, made of metal or more often of terracotta, discovered both on the island of Crete (Knossos, Gournia) and on the mainland (Delphi), seem to indicate that the form was widely distributed during the most flourishing period of the Minoan civilization (seventeenth-sixteenth centuries). It can be presumed that they were employed for votive rites like their counterparts in the form of complete animals, examples of which have come to light both in Crete and on the mainland.

The anomalous character of the object and the scarcity of similar finds on the continent leads to the belief that all such vessels were of Cretan origin and this assumption is even greater than for other painted, carved and embossed objects unearthed in the tombs or palaces of Mycenae, Tiryns and, generally speaking, in

Right
MYCENAEAN ARTIST
Rhyton, Head of a Lion
Sixteenth century B.C.
Embossed gold; height 7⅞″.
From Mycenae. (273)

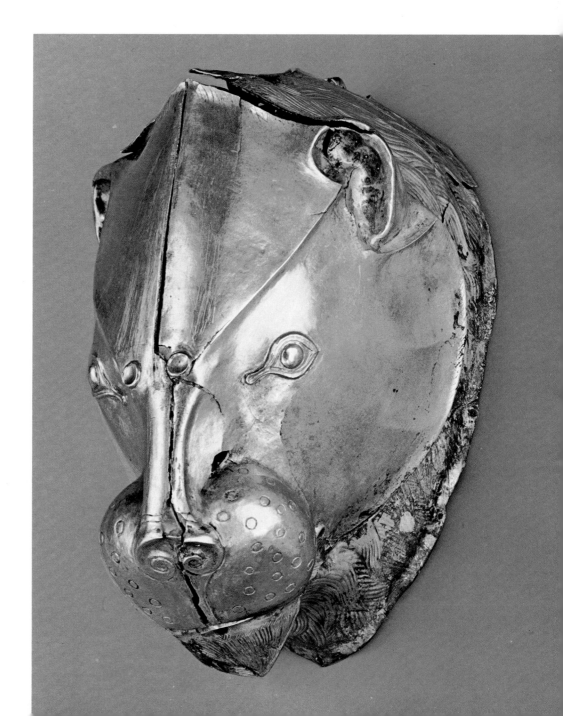

all of the Peloponnesos. The hypothesis of direct importation of Minoan art objects into the last-named region has for some time now been accompanied by the conviction that an indigenous culture, even if linked by strong contacts with Crete, began to flourish in southern Greece as early as the seventeenth century B.C. The majority of the extraordinary objects discovered by Heinrich Schliemann from 1876 onward must therefore be attributed to Greek artists.

MYCENAEAN CULTURE. *Rhyton, Head of a Lion.*   *p. 31*
Like the preceding object, this is also a ritual vessel in the form of an animal's head, but here a lion in embossed gold with evident formal analogies to the gold masks found in the Mycenaean tombs (from Tomb 4).

The austerely functional structure, the sobriety and the precision of this piece are in sharp contrast, however, with the naturalistic freedom of the preceding Cretan rhyton. It is for this reason, in fact, that we can say that it was a product of Greek soil, and this attribution is confirmed by the affinity of technique and inspiration with the gold masks.

MYCENAEAN CULTURE. *Bronze Daggers: Archers and Hoplites Hunting Lions; Leopard Attacking Ducks in a Pond.*   *p. 33*
Among the most fascinating articles found by Schliemann (1876) in the tombs excavated within the fortified walls of the Acropolis of Mycenae are these daggers inlaid with gold, silver and niello. The historical importance of this documentary treasure, as well as other similar objects found at later dates and other localities, is still the subject of discussion and contrasting explanations. The prevailing hypothesis today is that these explicitly Cretan forms, even if modified in varying stylistic ways, were the result of the diffusion of Minoan civilization across the Aegean Sea and its numerous small islands to the Peloponnesian coast; they are not, as was formerly believed, original documents of Cretan art imported into Greece.

The decorative technique of these daggers was complex. The little gold and silver figures were inlaid in a strip of dark enameled niello ground incrusted down the center of the bronze blade. The figures were then engraved, giving great graphic and chromatic liveliness to the scenes depicted: one showing a leopard attacking ducks in a papyrus swamp; another, hoplites and archers fighting a lion that is crushing under foot a wounded soldier, while two other infuriated beasts are shown in rapid flight.

The scenes are depicted with compositional resourcefulness, notably in the adaptation of the figures to the diminishing space. It has been justifiably observed that the same problem was mastered by the Greek sculptors a thousand years later, in the pediments of the monumental temples of the classical era.

Egyptian influence has often been observed in the figurations of this type, which recall scenes with papyri, flowers and animals along riverbanks such as are depicted, for example, in the Theban tomb now in the British Museum or in the tomb of Chenotep at Beni-Hassan.

These daggers are preserved in the Athens Museum together with two others found at the same time in Mycenae and a further pair from a tholos near Pylos.

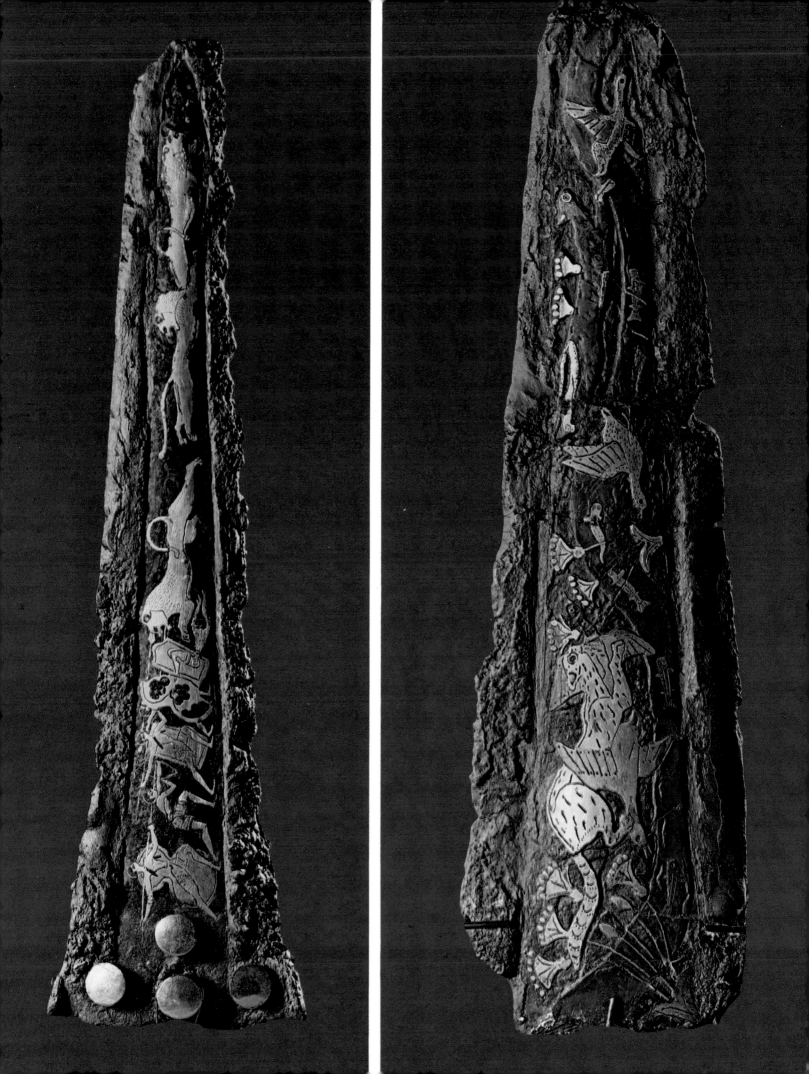

P. 35
MYCENAEAN CULTURE
Mask of a Prince
Sixteenth century B.C.
Gold; height 11⅞".
From Mycenae. (259)

MYCENAEAN CULTURE. *The So-called Mask of Agamemnon,*
and Mask of a Prince.   *pp. 36, 35*
These gold masks, together with others, from Shaft-Graves 4 and 5 of Mycenae,
were discovered by Schliemann, who believed that one (p. 36) was a portrait of
the great Homeric king.

It appears beyond a doubt today that these precious objects were native
creations of Greek civilization, rather than importations from Crete. In the first
place, it does not appear to have been customary in sixteenth-century Crete to
apply a portrait of the deceased to the sarcophagus or burial covering (an
obvious derivation from Egyptian funerary ritual); secondly, contrary toCretan
usage, gold was employed lavishly in the funerary apparatus of Mycenae,
proving that it was a custom peculiar to Hellenic cultures. The temptation to
recognize in these masks the features of Homeric heroes—even though they
lived three centuries later—appears comprehensible given their emphatic
characterization.

Although it has been frequently stated that the history of portraiture in
Western art begins with these masks, we cannot ignore the fact that there exist
large expressive and formalistic differences in these two works such as to make it
impossible to include both in a generic category. The so-called mask of
Agamemnon (p. 36), with its closed eyes, has an undoubted power to suggest
personality, but the stylized ears as well as the emphasized symmetries and shiny
surface confer a high degree of stylization on the work. The other mask (p. 35),
even though it follows the criteria of a preconceived style—note the flattened
ears—is completely different with its outright baldness, its large hairless face, its
bulging eyes completely closed by the eyelids and its still ironically sneering
mouth. Without being either a cast or a matrix, this head has the incisive, almost
aggressive, vitality of an exceptional personality.

P. 36
MYCENAEAN CULTURE
The So-called Mask of Agamemnon
Sixteenth century B.C.
Gold; height 8".
From Mycenae. (624)

MINOAN CULTURE
Hunters in a Chariot Attacking a Stag
Gold signet ring; height 1".
From Mycenae. (241)

MINOAN CULTURE. *Hunters Attacking a Stag from a Chariot.*
A series of gold signet rings discovered at Mycenae dating from the sixteenth century clearly belong to the tradition of Cretan toreutics. Even if these examples may actually have been executed by a mainland Greek master, they derive directly from Cretan art.

The extraordinary impetus given to the racing horses in this piece—in a horizontal movement paralleling the undulating lines of the ground below, which evokes a natural setting—together with the sudden swerve of the frightened stag, are the principal elements of the composition, even more than the small human figures engraved with incisive synthesis. They confer on the scene that dynamic quality peculiar to Cretan goldwork which distinguishes it from the contemporary production in Egypt and the Middle East in general.

These diminutive masterpieces—like those of other ancient civilizations characterized by closed, privileged, aristocratic societies—impose on the observer strict concentration. The unique virtue of this extremely stenographic and concise type of engraving is its visually bivalent quality: depending on the depth of the relief and the variations of light and shadow, the engraved surfaces produce the effect of intensifying the movement which, in the muscular bodies and the outlines of this piece foreshadows the bursts of energy of Antonio Pollaiuolo's athletic nudes.

MINOAN CULTURE. *Ornamental Embossed Disks.* p. 38–39
These small disks made from thin leaves of gold embossed with various stylized designs—palm leaves, spirals, rosettes, a butterfly—were believed by Heinrich Schliemann, who found 701 of them, to be ornamental studs for clothing. More probably they were used to decorate the winding-sheets or the sarcophagi which, like those used for Egyptian mummies, enclosed the embalmed bodies of the personages interred in the magnificent tombs of sixteenth-century Mycenae. The lack of any indication of a hole that would be necessary for attaching them as ornaments on peploi or mummies, and some traces of glue on the backs,

suggests that they were decorations applied to the wooden caskets or funerary cloths of the dead. Altogether, these light scintillating ornaments reflect the iconic and graphic fantasy of the artists who created them. A vast number of disks stamped in series, with a predilection for mobile rotating motifs, repeat symmetrical designs representing marine fauna or insects composed with ingenious variations. The afterlife of the deceased, at least that of the upper classes, was thus endowed with objects of daily use, of the same high aesthetic quality as was enjoyed during life in the buildings, the frescoes and the pottery.

MINOAN (?) CULTURE
Ornamental Embossed Disks
Sixteenth century B.C.
Gold; diams. 2"–2¾".
From Mycenae. (2,4,6,8–14)

MYCENAEAN CULTURE. *Stele of Departure for the Hunt.*   *p. 40*
This stele was originally located on Tomb no. 5 of the Acropolis of Mycenae. With its gravely damaged counterparts—the so-called "hunting scenes"—it was for a long time regarded as the first example of "monumental sculpture" in the history of Western art. Belonging to the earliest period of Mycenaean art, the summary and simplified character of its execution—so different from the masterly skill of the coeval goldsmiths—has been attributed to a lack of preceding experience in the medium: the Cretan artists did not carve in stone.

Even if we concede that it is not a work of outstanding quality, the difference between it and the contemporary toreutic art should be ascribed mainly to the adoption of different formalistic criteria. The stele has a precise architectonic structure, resulting from the equivalence of the two indentically framed panels. In the upper part the artist took up once again the ancient motif of interlocking spirals and emphasized the static value of the large intervening spaces with their four starlike points. In the lower part the directional movement conferred by the animal and the inclination of the drawn cart is integrated in a network of triangulations that immobilizes the whole group within parallels and rhythmically repeated figurations. The relief is deliberately contained within static limits and as such was carved in coherent separate compartments.

MINOAN (?) ARTIST. *Fragment of Vase with Battle Scene.*   *p. 41*
This is the largest surviving fragment of a remarkable document: a magnificent silver vase with gold rim and knobs, from one of the royal tombs of Mycenae. In its original state the uninterrupted scene on the body of the vase was quite complex: a city under siege situated on the slope of a hill thickly covered with trees; and city walls and towers from the heights of which the women spur on warriors fighting with primitive fury. Yet this figurative rendering does not exclude a supreme elegance of rhythmic poses and gestures, as if the participants were involved in a dance.

The reduction of this extraordinary masterpiece to a series of small fragments is one of the great losses of ancient art, yet these remains are sufficient to prove the existence of a supremely powerful artist. According to many archeologists, he was most probably Cretan, as evidenced by his love of life and drama,

Left
MYCENAEAN CULTURE
Stele of Departure for the Hunt
Sixteenth century B.C.
Calcareous tufa; 52⅜ × 41¾".
From Mycenae. (1428)

together with a Homeric power of expression manifested in the abrupt foreshortening of the landscape, and in the explosion of the groups and the figures linked together by continuous lines of tension. It is a presentation like no other, allowing us to relive a violent episode of primordial humanity.

Right
MINOAN(?) ARTIST
Fragment of Vase with Battle Scene, detail
Sixteenth century B.C.
Silver; height 3⅞"
(below, reconstructed vase:
height 8⅝", diam. 4½").
From Mycenae. (481)

MINOAN CULTURE. *Flying Fish.* *below*

Fresco painting was most probably introduced into Crete from Egypt at the apogee of the latter's artistic influence (1800–1500 B.C.). In Crete, however, it was characterized by "new" and original themes even as compared with Middle Eastern painting of the same period; in fact, its subjects and forms were derived from its flourishing art of pottery.

This fresco came to light at Phylakopi on the island of Melos and is precious proof of the diffusion of Minoan civilization in the Peloponnesos and the Cyclades. It takes up once again with renewed imagination the theme of a famous and fortunately still preserved fresco of the sixteenth century: the flying fish and dolphins painted on the walls of the queen's megaron (rectangular reception hall) in the palace at Knossos.

Both the representations and above all the expressive language will be found again in contemporary (1600–1500 B.C.) vases as well as on pottery of a later date. The dance of the flying fish in a sea criss-crossed by shadows and illuminated by rays of light is an unrestrained hymn to pure beauty and the joy of life which was to be rarely repeated with this particular emotional accent of triumphant discovery.

P. 43, above
MINOAN (?) ARTIST
Cup with the Capture of the Bulls
Fifteenth century B.C.
Gold; height 3¼"; diam. 4".
From Vapheio. (1758)

P. 43, below
MINOAN (?) ARTIST
Cup with Grazing Bulls
Fifteenth century B.C.
Gold; height 3⅛"; diam. 4".
From Vapheio. (1759)

Below
MINOAN CULTURE
Flying Fish, fragments
Sixteenth century B.C.
Fresco; height 9".
From Phylakopi. (5844)

MINOAN ARTIST. *Cup with the Capture of the Bulls;
Cup with Grazing Bulls.*   *p. 43*

Although for a long time these two cups found at Vapheio near Sparta in
Lakonia have been defined as masterpieces of Cretan art, there is a tendency
today to attribute them to the wider sphere of Minoan civilization. It is
presumed, in other words, that they were the work of Cretan goldsmiths
emigrated to the Peloponnesos or that they were imported from the island.

The two cups of more or less identical form and dimensions, in which the
same technique of embossing and expert chasing was employed, depict two
moments of a single event in a tree-shaded pastoral landscape. The first,
portraying the struggles of the beasts with the man, presents the observer with
continuous motifs of torsion and movement, expressions of savage violence and
indomitable rebellion; in the second, illustrating the subdued beasts taken to
pasture, the outlines of the animals are characterized by amply paced rhythmic
cadences.

The two scenes are based on an antithesis of subject matter: one, the hunt,
capture and taming of the animals, which are notable for their violence; the

MYCENAEAN CULTURE
Head of a Woman
Fifteenth century B.C.
Stuccoed and painted calcareous stone;
height 6¼".
From Mycenae. (4575)

44

other, an episode of idyllic life under trees. They are expressions of an inspiration that embraces both the epic and the lyrical.

The powerful vision, which maintains an actuality that is beyond time in its spontaneous feeling of solidarity with living nature, is developed by the visual rotating movement that achieves an exceptional intensity in such figures as the roaring bull ensnared in the net.

These gold cups from Vapheio, together with the silver vase of the battle scene from Mycenae (p. 41), reach a culminating point of artistic expression in the emotional intensity of a supreme art.

MYCENAEAN CULTURE. *Head of a Woman.* p. 44

In the total absence of important surviving sculpture, this painted head is the only example of plastic art in full round we have inherited from Mycenae, where it was found. As was the case with the stele of the preceding century (p. 40), the interest in plastic investigation is to be found in the construction of planes in a synthetically powerful volume, on a principle analogous to that used for vase-forms. The crown of hair, the sharp line of the ribbon on the forehead, the oval eye-sockets and indentations around the mouth, the long ridge of the nose and the prominent chin all emphasize the geometric conception. The latter is stressed further by the symmetrical positioning on the cheeks and chin of the curious and otherwise anomalous motif of little red flowers, which has induced some archeologists to consider this to be the head of a sphinx. Compared with other products of Mycenaean art, this head obviously has a completely different character from the lively works in metal, terracotta and fresco associated with the Minoan civilization; according to some students it should be attributed to the thirteenth century B.C.

MYCENAEAN ARTIST. *Ring with Homage of Demons to a Goddess.* below

This gold signet ring is one of the most important objects found in the remarkable material brought to light in the royal tombs of Mycenae and Tiryns documenting the particular character of Cretan and Mycenaean art. It was

MYCENAEAN ARTIST
Ring with Homage of Demons to a Goddess.
Fifteenth century B.C.
Gold signet ring; height 2¼".
From Tiryns. (6208)

discovered in the excavation of the Palace of Tiryns and was part of the so-called "Tiryns Treasure," generally dated from the fifteenth century B.C.

The abundance of symbols and allusive elements it contains makes it extremely valuable for a study of the religion and customs of Mycenean culture in the fifteenth-fourteenth centuries. Special attention has been focused on the precision with which clothing and articles of daily use are represented. It has generally been considered a depiction of a propitiatory ceremony against the drought of summer in the parched fields of the Peloponnesos.

A crowned female figure seated in an orchard, clothed in a bell-shaped dress and holding a rhyton accepts as homage the offerings contained in long-necked wine vessels *(oinochoi)* brought by four demonic figures—half-beast, half-insect. The meaning is obscure, but the engraving is vivid and incisive, with great attention paid to the compositional arrangement and the rhythmic repetition of the figures.

MYCENAEAN CULTURE
Head of a Lady
Ca. 1400 B.C.
Fresco; height 7½".
From Tiryns. (5883)

MYCENAEAN CULTURE. *Head of a Lady.*   *p. 47*
As in Crete, the vast walls of the megaron (reception hall), such as existed in the palaces of Mycenae, Tiryns, Thebes and Ano Englianos, offered ample space for mural decoration. The walls were subdivided into geometric panels in which animal, battle, or hunting scenes were portrayed; but there were also series of panels depicting processions of male and female figures (mostly the latter) directly derived from analogous paintings at Knossos.

This detail is one of the largest among the numerous fragments from a *Procession of Maidens* found in the Palace of Tiryns and dating from about 1400 or a decade or so later. The figures are shown in profile and in single file but are divided into two facing columns, as if converging (most probably) on a divinity, of which no fragment remains. As in Cretan frescoes, there is a delicate deep-blue background bordered at the top by a frieze of rosettes and ribbons; the base consists of a socle decorated with vertical red and blue bands surmounted by a larger section simulating a wooden floor. Comparing this figure with the head from Mycenae (p. 44) one immediately notes the similiarity of the headdress, the oblique eyes, the elongated nose, and also the difference in the elaboration of the same profile in the undulating rhythm of the decorative friezes of the Tiryns fresco.

MYCENAEAN CULTURE. *Three-handled Hydria with Palmette Motif.*   *p. 48*
The stylized palmettes as well as the centrally arranged lance-shaped motifs decorating this hydria (large water jar) are characteristic of the "First Palace Style" of Cretan pottery. This jar, found at Deiras near Argos, indicates that the process of orderly stylization occurring in Minoan vases spread to the continent during the course of the fifteenth and fourteenth centuries. The well-spaced, symmetrically and rigidly ordered ornament of this vase, like the friezes of the palace frescoes, acquired around 1400 B.C. a particular character of deliberately restrained elegance. It is typical of numerous finds of analogous ceramic objects that they were without doubt the products of a workshop similar to the one in the so-called Cadmos Palace of the ancient Theban Acropolis, found with its kilns and working materials still intact.

MYCENAEAN CULTURE
Three-handled Hydria with Palmette Motif
Fifteenth-fourteenth century B.C.
Terracotta; height 17¾".
From Deiras. (1707)

MYCENAEAN CULTURE. *Grave Stele with Painted Warriors and Does.*   *p. 49*

The two frescoed panels on this large but poorly preserved fragment of a grave stele of the fourteenth century, were clearly inspired by the oldest Cretan mural paintings. Both the human figures and the animals—deer, does and a porcupine—are aligned in profile, and framed in vertical and horizontal borders containing a curving, concentric, overlapping motif. As far as can be judged today, the colors even in their original state must have been quite simple: ochre, red, black and blue-green applied to a monochrome background analogous to that of vase painting. The result evidently emphasizes the taste for simplification that inspired the deliberate repetition of the movement of the protagonists in single file, and determined the absence of any detail suggesting environment or of any other possible allusion.

It has been noted that the stele was at first simply engraved and only painted at a later date, with a technique that was similar to that used for pottery. In fact,

P. 49
MYCENAEAN CULTURE
Grave Stele with Painted Warriors and Does
Fourteenth century B.C.
Fresco on terracotta; height 36".

with this object we are once again faced with a work of art which has no relation to Minoan culture; it is an example of a production—especially of ceramics—that was located in Mycenae, Cyprus or elsewhere. It is characterized by a keen sensitivity to, and penetrating investigation of, compositional rhythm; and the latter was accompanied by a spontaneity of imagery that at times could be defined as gross, "popular," or even childish, and yet at the same time extemporaneously and pungently ironic and caricatural.

MYCENAEAN ARTIST. *Warrior Krater.*   *below*
Discovered by Schliemann in an interior chamber of the lower part of the Acropolis of Mycenae—the so-called "House of the Warrior Vase"—this large libation bowl or vase is a characteristic product of the final phase of Mycenaean culture (thirteenth century B.C.). It repeats in a very close fashion the figuration

MYCENAEAN ARTIST
The Warrior Krater
Thirteenth century B.C.
Terracotta; height 16⅛"; diam. 19⅛".
From Mycenae. (1426)

of the panels of the preceding painted stele, a subject that was quite evidently a favorite with several artists of the period commonly called "Mycenaean III C," and was widely dispersed, as indicated by the presence in Rome (Palazzo dei Conservatori) of the Krater of Aristhonotos, brought to light at Caere.

The design of warriors marching in file with legs like calipers, together with the vertical parallels of their bodies and the slanting parallels of their lances deliberately repeated, creates an obvious and emphatic rhythmic movement. The figures are drawn without any attempt to beautify but with a spontaneous improvisation that excludes any calligraphic or purely decorative intentions. The phenomenon was common to various Mycenaean centers in the Mediterranean and reflects a desire for artistic independence and originality.

MYCENAEAN CULTURE. *Vase with Warriors, Chariot and Dogs* (fragment). *below*

In this precious fragment from Tiryns, even better than in some of the less deteriorated objects (pp. 44–50), we can note the extraordinary freedom of imagination and the bold creative impulse of the Greek potters of the late Mycenaean period. Every motif derived from nature is disarranged and decomposed only to be reorganized in threadlike, pearl-like, serpentine, interwoven or striped ornamental forms.

The artist organized these improbable bodies, these outlines reminiscent of savage prehistoric figures and masks, with a compositional and repetitive rigor that re-interpreted forms of expression typical of the earliest period of Cretan-Mycenaean art. Noteworthy are the calculated rhythms of the horizontal and vertical lines of the human and animal bodies and even the chariot, together with the rhythm of the outlines and the striped surface, which, in turn, are repeated in the decorative spirals of the background.

MYCENAEAN ARTIST. *Head of Warrior.*   *below*

Ivory carving, widely adopted on the Greek mainland even for articles of daily use, had no known precedents in Minoan art; but the discovery of ivory sculptures in the Peloponnesos indicates that its use was rather frequent there, beginning as early as the fifteenth century B.C. The ascertained origin of the material in Syria and the known commercial relations with both Palestine and

MYCENAEAN ARTIST
Head of Warrior
Thirteenth century (?) B.C.
Ivory; height 4⅜".
(2648)

P. 53
MYCENAEAN ARTIST
Two Goddesses and a Divine Child
Thirteenth century (?) B.C.
Ivory; height 3¼".
From Mycenae. (7711)

52

Syria are convincing evidence that this established form of artistic expression must be attributed to examples imported from the Middle East which exerted an influence on Greece. Cyprus was likewise affected, where the production of ivories survived to an even later date. The existing examples, moreover, are indicative of an artistic activity that we shall never be able to know or understand because the most fragile items have disappeared, namely carving and sculpture in wood, which unquestionably must have existed.

This warrior's head with a type of helmet which is distinctively, Mycenaean is attributed by many students to an exceedingly late period, the thirteenth century. The sculpture is dominated by the same architectonic-volumetric criteria that inspired the production of objects of daily use as well as armor such as helmets and breastplates. The head, the ears, and the headdress are also characterized by the pure formalism of the circles and the jointed links of the armor.

MYCENAEAN ARTIST. *Two Goddesses and a Divine Child.*   *p. 53*
This ivory group, discovered in a Mycenaean sanctuary in 1939, has aroused enormous iconographical interest due to the presence of the two "mothers" united at the back by the daring swath of the peplos, offering protection and comfort to a child divinity playing at the knees of the two female figures. It is a sort of divine "trinity" which has no other known counterpart. Even in this complex and elaborate example of ivory sculpture one notes the attention paid to giving a precise historical character to the costume which in this particular case is Minoan. Although believed by some experts to be older, this ivory is generally dated as a product of the thirteenth century B.C.

Taking into account its tiny dimensions, this work is a masterpiece of rhythmic composition inspired by a refined feeling for sculptural light and shade, achieved through an extremely flexible, resourceful technique.

MYCENAEAN ARTIST
Female Figure
Thirteenth century B.C.
Fragment of fresco.
From Mycenae.

MYCENAEAN ARTIST. *Female Figure.*   *p. 55*
This superb fragment of a mural painting was recently discovered (1970) in a house inside the western wall of the Acropolis of Mycenae. The splendid figure—which has been called the "Mycenaean Woman"—is characterized by audacity and originality even within a continuity of style in the clothing and headdress. It is, therefore, one of the most precious documents from the end of the Mycenaean era. It has been attributed to the thirteenth century.

The lovely face is seen in profile, but the bust—and presumably the entire figure—is depicted frontally. The hands move gracefully, one holding a necklace (or are they snakes?), in what seems to be a rhythmic dance as indicated by the curving borders of the gown that move in various directions. If there were not objective archeological reasons for not dating this painting several centuries after the Minoan-Mycenaean period, the similarity of clothing with that of later sculpture might tempt us to compare it with the latter as a document of completely independent inspiration and form.

ATTIC ARTIST. *Funerary Amphora of the Dipylon.* *p. 57*

Following the declining tradition of figurative art in the Peloponnesos, there was a long break, between 1200 and 900 B.C., during which the flourishing life of the Mycenaean strongholds was replaced by a period of difficult life—the historical era of the Trojan War and the afflictions of returning warriors—characterized by devastating invasions and undeniable poverty. It was an epoch of general crisis for the entire civilized world, devoid of any sign of real originality in the production of art objects for either ritual or daily use.

The discoveries made in the large necropolis of the Dipylon (cemetery with two entrances) on the Elysian road at the gates of Athens document this phase in a tedious repetition of ancient traditional formulas; but they also bear the first signs of a revival of creative activity in Greece and Athens in particular, which was one of the last of the Mycenaean citadels to be constructed and which had emerged unscathed from the disastrous events that had destroyed the other cities of the Greek continent. This rebirth, it is believed, began during the ninth century B.C. Modern research has made it possible to follow in an unbroken line the figurative development of the so-called "poor" or sub-Mycenaean ceramics as well as of the more elaborate "protogeometric" Attic pottery. The overall picture supplied by ever-increasing documentation is extremely complex, however, and consists of long periods in which Mycenaean cultural influences persisted, mixed nevertheless with other stimuli arising from new contacts and knowledge.

The Dipylon preserved some of the finest examples of the potter's art of ancient Attica, which during the eighth century was to produce some of the most

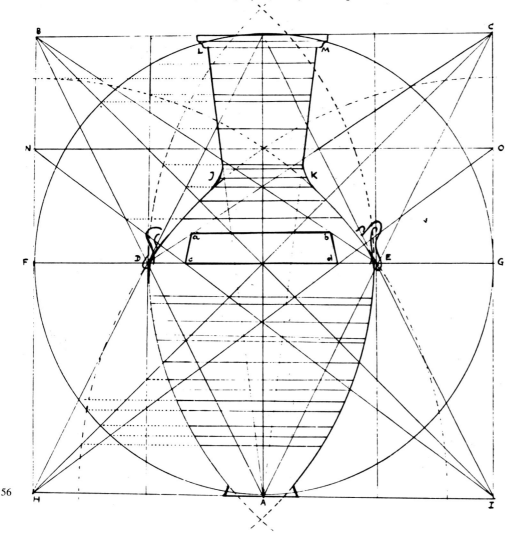

56

ATTIC ARTIST
Funerary Amphora of the Dipylon
Eighth century B.C.
Terracotta; height (with restored foot) 61″.
From the Dipylon. (804)
Left: Schematic drawing illustrating the architectonic structure of the amphora (C.L. Ragghianti).

remarkable creations of Greek civilization. First among many as regards quality, if not age, is this *Funerary Amphora of the Dipylon* on which the vast decorative network is developed with a concise discipline and almost musical rhythm which enhance the form of this colossal vase. This monumental vase served as a *sema* or indicator placed above the grave even though the custom of cremation had been abandoned. The bands of geometric motifs, suggestively augmenting and diminishing in width, give choral support to the large central scene of *The Mourned* which is also characterized by repetitive rhythms, although employed with greater compositional freedom. Even the narrow bands on the neck, one near the top and one at its base, where the repeated outlines of tiny animals replace in an imaginative formula the variations of the meander pattern—the windings, rhombi, checkerboards, and crosses that definitively supplanted the circular motifs—give a refined and erudite emphasis to the importance of the central scene.

The drawing reproduced on p. 56 (Ragghianti, 1952) illustrates the rigorous architectonic composition of the decoration; similar reconstructions could be made of other urns from the Dipylon. Within the fundamental module of the square-circle the artist traced a continuous and correlated series of connections and unitary relationships which not only regulate all the bands of the annular decoration but also the position and dimensions of the prothesis (panel of *The Mourned*), while the vertical elements emphasize the generating lines of the form and proportions of the vase. It is a remarkable illustration of that ratio or science of the rules which, parallel to the Greek rhetoric and logical system, created the essential character of Hellenic art as it has been transmitted to us throughout the centuries. The structure of this type of amphora clearly indicates that it was the work of masters who had the same intellectual capacity, and employed the same formulas, as the architects who built the temples and the theaters.

GREEK ARTIST. *Striped Oinochoe with Inscription.* *p. 59*
This wine pitcher is an invaluable document because an inscription scratched on it is in the most ancient Greek language known to us. The pitcher can be dated from the second half of the eighth century B.C. and proves that the making of purely geometrically decorated pottery was still very much a current activity, as can be seen also in many other examples of post-Mycenaean culture found in the Dipylon cemetery. The inscription reads: "The dancer who dances best will receive this vase." The concise figuration on the neck depicts a fawn and a bird enclosed within zigzag lines that were inspired by the overall geometric pattern. This oinochoe, with its clearly modulated graphic system distributed in conformity with the form, is decorated on the upper part with a wide black band and in the lower half by an animated alternation of wide and narrow bands.

ATTIC ARTIST. *Funerary Krater with Prothesis and Procession of Chariots.* *p. 60*
The great ceramist who was the creator of this famous krater was close both in language and in time to the master of the Dipylon (pp. 56, 57). Presumably a little younger, he is now considered to have been the founder of the school of "Geometric" pottery. As can be seen in this vase, the younger man invented a

GREEK ARTIST
Striped Oinochoe with an Inscription
Eighth century B.C.
Terracotta; height 8⅝".
From the Dipylon. (192)

192

variation on the general architectonic structure with a more truncated and concentrated pattern. He multiplied the choral scenes (prothesis) by utilizing the area within the indented eyebrow-shaped handles and by extending the procession of chariots around the entire equatorial line of the vase. The dominating geometric pattern emphasizes the human or animal figures and the objects whose schematic value is defined functionally by the recurring rhythms of the overall conception.

CYCLADIC ARTIST. *Krater with Horsemen (Abduction of Iole?).*   below
This krater is characteristic of the vases produced in the Cycladic islands during the eighth century B.C. Exceptional in its perfect condition, it bears the images of horsemen facing one another, Herakles abducting Iole(?) and, on the neck, Hermes and Alkestis(?). Found on the island of Melos, it is generally dated about 750 B.C. The dominating decorative motif is the lotus flower geometrized into four joined coils which appear both on the neck of the vase and inserted

MASTER OF THE VILLARD VASE
Amphora with Chariot Race
Eighth century B.C.
Terracotta; height 30¼″
(with cover, 35⅜″.)
(894)

between the horsemen-protagonists of the wide middle band. The profusion of embellishing palmettes, spiral scrolls, rhombi and triangles that fill even the background of the principal scene makes this vase a spectacular example of the tendency toward overall ornamentation that was particularly noticeable in the eighth century pottery of the Aegean islands. The form of the krater is original: it is fundamentally divided into four sections that develop on the axis of two wedged cones; the friezes are confined to the upper and lower sections, while the larger median area is reserved for the scenes with the figures. The dominating geometric criterion of decoration was modified here, and this krater was thus a foreshadowing of later ceramics concentrating more explicitly on human and animal figurations. The graphic motifs and the rhythmic repetition indicate a clear relationship with artistic forms of eastern Mediterranean cultures.

MASTER OF THE VILLARD VASE. *Amphora with Chariot Race.*   *p. 62*

The potter who produced this monumental amphora with a lid decorated with the funerary symbol of the serpent in relief is named after the expert who identified the style of several works in the collections of the Louvre: F. Villard. The more "classic" phase of the Geometric era, which presumably lasted several decades around the middle of the eighth century, was followed toward the close of the century by a period of search for increased freedom and dexterity that was almost a reaction to the constructive severity of the magnificent models of the Master of the Dipylon and his immediate successors.

The graphic solution of the friezes of this amphora, in which a chariot race is depicted, is less solid and rigorous, especially as regards the human figures. There are now variations in the dominating rhythms of the rows of chariots, quadrigae and marching warriors. A tendency to roughly outline is also evident, and the alignment of the decorative and figured bands themselves is carried out with a far less rigid symmetry.

ATTIC ARTIST. *Nude Goddess with Diadem.*   *p. 64*

This is the most refined and expressive of five analogous small ivory statues that twentieth-century critics date from 770 B.C. at the earliest. They are the coeval counterpart in another medium, also of very high quality, of the investigations and formalistic aspirations of the Master of the Dipylon. In fact, they were brought to light in the Kerameikos (pottery section) of the Dipylon and in the same tomb that contained the precious "Geometric" vases.

The sacerdotal attitude and the nudity of the divinity—which are quite evidently of Middle Eastern inspiration—prove how the artists of Attica during the first half of the eighth century interpreted and assimilated with great originality forms that had become known to them through historically documented contacts with neighboring contemporary civilizations.

GREEK ARTIST. *Statuette of Warrior with Conical Cap, or Helmet (?).*   *p. 65*

In the triangular definition of the body and the mechanical gestures of this small-scale sculpture it is customary to recognize a product of the same "Geometric" period as the previous item; but at the same time in the increased anatomical articulation can also be seen an impairment of the equilibrium and simplification characteristic of this type of art. It is for this reason that small bronzes of this type can be dated with all probability from the end of the eighth century B.C. One should also take note of an analogous, mutilated bronze—no. 6612 in the same museum—wherein the arms are even more clearly bent toward the body in a less angular, more natural movement.

ATTIC ARTIST
Nude Goddess with Diadem
Eighth century B.C.
Ivory; height 9¾".
From the Dipylon. (776)

GREEK ARTIST
Statuette of Warrior with Conical Cap
Eighth century B.C.
Bronze; height 7⅞″.
(6613)

ARTIST OF THE PELOPONNESOS. *Clytemnestra stabbing Cassandra.*

p. 67

This bronze relief found in the Heraion of Argos and portraying the Achaean queen in the act of killing her rival, the Trojan princess, was originally probably a panel of a tripod. Clytemnestra, who is smaller, advances from the left toward her victim whom she grabs by the hair, and holding her firmly, stabs her in the loins. It is a scene of lucid and pitiless iciness that has few counterparts in all art. The triangulated composition of the arms and gestures that unites the two figures of the tragic encounter emphasizes the incisiveness of the drama. The headdresses with long curls studded with pearls, the network of small disks on the gowns and the braided decorative border are all clearly oriental in inspiration. The figures, embossed and engraved with trenchant graphic technique, have counterparts in certain bronze laminae from Olympia of the eighth-seventh centuries and even in some figurations of paleo-Venetian art brought to light in the area around Bologna and Este.

ARTIST OF THE PELOPONNESOS
Clytemnestra Stabbing Cassandra
Seventh century B.C.
Embossed and engraved bronze lamina; height 18⅛".
From Argos. (15131)

ARTIST OF BOEOTIA. *Quadriga with Two Warriors.*

p. 68

This is a fine example of the flourishing and widespread production of small terracotta sculptures in Boeotia where the traditional Geometric style of the earlier bronze art of Attica continued for a longer period of time—during the entire seventh century—although it became more animated and was rejuvenated through orientalizing influences.

Generally speaking such small groups of figures portray—with the same techniques and formalistic solutions as the archaic bronzes—moments, objects, situations and episodes of daily life; yet it must be noted that they have a natural spontaneity that approximates innocent simplicity. Given the complexity of the subject matter and the composition—such as in this quadriga—it might seem that there was an underlying taste and desire for exemplification on a more grandiose scale. In any case the overall structure, the interrelationship of the parts and the rhythm of the whole express an authoritativeness that goes beyond "popular" art.

ANALOTOS PAINTER. *Three-Handled Amphora with Confronted Lions.*

p. 69, left

The oversize figures predominating over the geometric decorations of the subdividing panels, together with the modules full of red and white touches enlivening the images, make this one of the finest and most typical examples of Attic pottery from the beginning of the seventh century, when certain architectonic principles of the previous tradition were still being respected; i.e., the sharp subdivision of the horizontal bands; the importance of outlines in the geometric composition (as on the vases of the Dipylon); the correlation of the movement with the rhythms of space. Quite correctly the artist—called the Analotos Painter after the place where this amphora was found—is now considered the founder of the so-called "Proto-Attic" school of potters. He proves to have been the protagonist of the passage to the "new" conception that extended structural precedents by elaborating the form of the vase in such a way

as to enlarge the zones with figurative representations, and to contrast the visual mobility of the bands with the visual rigidity of the expanded space.

The principal motif consists of two confronted lions; their flexible, impetuous paws reach out against the large clear background in a trapezoidal opening which subtly reduces the space of the enclosing framework. Two series of minor figures—the four-footed, conventional, abstract animals in the lower band, and the freely drawn procession of male and female figures on the neck, in a festive or perhaps votive ceremony (indicated by the presence of garlands)—give a strong rhythmic impulse to the overall decorative composition.

ARTIST OF EUBOEA. *Amphora with Sphinx and Female Figures.*   *p. 69, right*
This magnificent example of the colossal ceramics produced in the first half of the seventh century in the Euboea area north of Thebes was found at Eretria and presumably was produced in a local kiln. Both its grandiose dimensions and its

ARTIST OF BOEOTIA
Quadriga with Two Warriors
Seventh century B.C.
Terracotta; height 8".
(4082)

Below left
PAINTER OF ANALOTOS
Three-handled Amphora with Confronted Lions
Seventh century B.C.
Terracotta; 30".
(313)

Below right
ARTIST OF EUBOEA
Amphora with Sphinx and Female Figures
Seventh century B.C.
Terracotta; height 30".
From Eretria. (12129)

exceptionally vast figurations were typical of that pottery: a series of female figures—whose spindly legs emerge like pairs of compasses from their rectangular peploi—in the band around the tall cylindrical neck; and the Sphinx—the sole protagonist on the swollen body of the vase—whose figuration is fused with the spirals, coils and rosettes which invade the uniform light background in harmony with the slow rhythm that characterizes the entire decoration.

CYCLADIC CULTURE. *Amphora with the Meeting of Apollo and*
the Muses with Artemis.   *below and detail right*
A series of monumental amphorae from Melos refer directly to the cult of
Apollo. The decoration is developed according to a tripartite scheme of wide
bands ornamented with lively spirals combined with animal, vegetable and
purely ornamental motifs. The fusion of the geometric frieze, of evident
Corinthian inspiration, with the curvilinear "orientalizing" ornamentation
remained one of the persistent features in the pottery of the Cycladic islands
during the entire seventh century (this amphora can be dated about 650 B.C.).

Within a definite stylization, the graphic style of this and other similar vases

Left, and detail right
CYCLADIC CULTURE
Amphora with the Meeting of Apollo and
the Muses with Artemis
Seventh century B.C.
Terracotta; height 37".
From Melos. (911)

is singularly free, as can be seen not only in the insertion of floral decoration in the triangular spaces between the legs of the four ambling, winged horses, but especially in the curving forms and the fanciful figuration drawn with provocative liveliness, as in the heads of the horses and the deer.

The form of this amphora—and other examples on Melos itself, at Eretria, in Boeotia and in Cyprus—consists of a cylindrical neck with sectionalized decoration, the body of the vase spherically dilated in the center, and the base formed by a double cone. This form makes it possible to obtain a series of stable pictorial panels which alternate with a generally mobile representation in the wider bands; the overall geometric effect is, therefore, quite original. (There is still much to be clarified regarding pottery forms, the various types of vases depending on the functions or uses for which they were intended. Ragghianti insists on the dynamics of the liquids as a primary condition.)

CORINTHIAN ARTIST. *Metope with Scene of the Myth of Chelidon and Aedon.* *p. 73*
This is one of two surviving metopes from the Temple of Apollo at Thermos in Aetolia that should be included among the few objects which can document the monumental painting known to have flourished and, in most cases, to have constituted an integral part of sacred architecture during the course of the seventh century B.C. Both metopes were painted by a Corinthian artist about 630 B.C.—the ascertained moment of artistic pre-eminence of that city, and of northern Greece. He isolated and exalted the figures of the protagonists, firmly enclosing them within large ornamental friezes, which contrasts with the decorative cramming so frequently found on the vases. The female figure in this panel is intensely emphasized and animated by the graphic rhythm. Note should be taken of the artist's interest in the profile, revealed by the beautifully modeled ear and the frontal position of the eye.

CYCLADIC ARTIST. *Krater with Herakles and Deianira.* *p. 74*
Another fine example of Cycladic pottery, also found on the island of Melos, is this krater in which the potter, perhaps of a slightly later period than the preceding, was inspired by a taste for more ancient Attic ceramics, as can be seen in his greater insistence on the division into compartments both of his figurative groups and his ornamental motifs. Coils, palmettes, spirals, stars and rosettes assume vast dimensions and are distributed over the surface of the vessel in spacing that is equivalent to that of the figures, in such a way as to become not only more evident but also more powerful elements. As compared with the preceding vase, the graphics of this krater are characterized, within the terms of a common culture, by a richer, more insistent search for stylization.

Unfortunately the vivid original polychrome colors—another important feature of this island pottery—have practically disappeared on this and the preceding vases, all superb survivors of a great art.

PELOPONNESIAN SCULPTOR. *Woman with Veil.* *p. 75*
Contrary to what has been asserted for a long time, some experts now doubt that this is one of the metopes that embellished the Doric temple which arose on the ruins of the royal palace of Mycenae. It seems probable, however, that this sculpture did actually come from the Peloponnesos and that it was the work of an artist of the seventh century (it has been dated ca. 625 B.C.). It is also evident that the sculptor took his inspiration directly from the Cretan figurative tradition—see the *Draped Woman* found in Auxerre and the *Necklace of Kamiros* in Rhodes—and from contemporary Corinthian sculpture. This

CORINTHIAN ARTIST
Metope with Scene of the Myth of Chelidon and Aedon
Seventh century B.C.
Fragment; height 17".
From Thermos. (13410)

CYCLADIC CULTURE
Krater with Hercules and Deianira
Seventh century B.C.
Terracotta; height 39⅜".
From Melos. (354)

association is not limited to certain typological aspects such as the triangular masses of the headdress or the tiny circles of curls on the forehead or the rigid and geometric (but humanly sensitive) features of this personage. Far more evident are the analogies, notably with the *Antefix* (Museum of Athens) from the Temple of Artemis at Kalydon, and its counterpart from Thermos. The observer should note the strong construction of the head placed on the cylindrical neck and framed by the heavy parallel bands. It was carved with loving care and humanized by the trace of a light smile on the fleshy lips. The falling and enveloping veil with a large single fold is an ellipse that counterbal-

PELOPONNESIAN SCULPTOR
Woman with Veil
Seventh century B.C.
Height 15 ¾".
(2869)

ances the ellipse of the wavy locks of hair, thus blocking in—as far as a reconstruction is possible—an outline of a pulsating oval enclosing the animated image.

PIRAEUS PAINTER. *Amphora with Chariots.*   *p. 77*
The name of the Attic potter who painted this remarkable amphora toward the end of the seventh century (ca. 620 B.C.) derives from the place where it was found. The large uninterrupted figuration on the body and the proud rooster on the neck were placed with extraordinary equilibrium in the spontaneity of the pictorial composition. Series of minute, mobile and alternating geometric motifs support the depiction of the chariots and the nervous horses, which are sketched in with such rapid incisiveness on the central band of the vase that many experts believe that it was one of the first examples of "black-figure" pottery.

    The distinction between red figures on a black background and black figures on a red or white background has been for a long time an essential method of classifying Greek vases. Yet there is more to it than that, and the system can be an oversimplification. The Piraeus painter to a great extent employed the technique of engraving—or *graffito*—to give life to his figures. The chrome black, therefore, was not applied smoothly, firmly and regularly; it is rippled and of unequal thicknesses varying with the drawing which, although respecting the triangular module of the pacing horses' legs, appears abrupt, fortuitous and accordingly animated by a spirited impulse.

PIRAEUS PAINTER
Amphora with Chariots
Seventh century B.C.
Terracotta; height 43¼".
From Piraeus. (353)

NESSOS PAINTER. *Amphora with the Duel Between Herakles and Nessos, and the Slaying of the Gorgon.*   *pp. 78–79*
This splendid example of the art of the seventh century was brought to light in the cemetery of the Dipylon. The two scenes occupy much of the space offered by the elongated body of the grandiose amphora from which the name of the painter (about 630 B.C.) has been derived. The decorative motifs are limited to thin bands on the base and the neck; small framed panels depicting fantastic birds were even inserted into the two large, solid handles. Without doubt the most extraordinary aspect of this masterpiece consists of the continuous figuration showing the bodies of the Gorgons pursuing the slayer of their sister: the monsters spread the deadly mass of their dark wings over the central part of the vase, while below the thin legs nimbly flex their joints, gradually lightening the images as they extend down toward the empty base. Only a few brief, light motifs break the continuity of the movement.

    This imposing, monumental work has been praised for the perfect balance of its structure: the harmonious stereometric construction has a rectangular, reticulated, geometric matrix in the center of which is traced the semicircle that defines the upper part of the vase; at the base it is constructed on the diameter according to the lines of an acute arc with external centers. The cylindrical neck curves inward in order to counter the outward flow of the shoulder of the body. This structure is accompanied by a similar composition of the figures and the groups and by the distribution of the decoration which is both musical and dramatic.

    As in the previous example, the painter resorted to engraving and graffito techniques; small incisive red brushstrokes—in part still visible—contribute to heightening the animation.

Left and detail right
NESSOS PAINTER
Amphora with the Duel Between Hercules and Nessos and the Slaying of the Gorgon
Ca. 630 B.C.
Terracotta; height 4'.
From the Dipylon. (1002)

ATTIC SCULPTOR. *Kouros of Sounion.*   *p. 80*

The significance and function of a large number of huge standing figures of nude youths (called kouroi) placed in the temples of Attica from the end of the seventh century onward, have not yet been definitively ascertained. Fortunately many of them have survived and amply document their creation and duration during the entire sixth century. They were not the object of some cult, yet in some way were connected with the divinities of the temple. The most common interpretation is the belief that they—together with companion figures of young women, called korai—were sculptures of the faithful dedicated to the gods.

This colossal figure from Cape Sounion is thought to have been set up originally in front of the Temple of Poseidon (Neptune) facing the sea; it is also considered the earliest example of its type, having been carved about the end of the seventh century. With other statues of kouroi it indicates access of Greek culture to Egyptian canons, such as had been elaborated as early as 3000 B.C. and amplified during the course of the seventh century. The module was 16.5 hands in height—originally 309.3750 centimeters—which corresponds to the Biton of Delphi, the work of Polymedes—and this is practically equal to the *Kouros* in the Metropolitan Museum of New York which has also been found identical with

P. 80
ATTIC SCULPTOR
Kouros of Sounion
End of seventh century
Marble; height 11⅜".
(3645)

Below, left
BOEOTIAN SCULPTOR
Head of Kouros from the Ptoion
End of seventh century B.C.
Stone; height 11½" (presumed
total height about 77").
From Orchomenos. (15)

Below, right
ATTIC SCULPTOR
Head of Kouros from the Dipylon
Ca. 610 B.C.
Height 1⅜" (total original ht. about 76").
From the Dipylon. (3372)

the Egyptian module. The principle of the Egyptian canon was architectonic: a statue, like architecture, should be produced in separate interchangeable parts without the slightest variation in dimensions, even if by two artists in two different and distant localities. Diodorus of Sicily makes note of this when writing about Telecles of Samos and Theodoros of Ephesos. Therefore to this geometric structural criterion we must attribute the polygonal composition of the chest, abdomen, hips and knees; the solely frontal aspect; the parallelism and symmetry of the arms and legs; the fixity of the frozen motion. The earlier experience, which culminated in the geometric culture of the Dipylon, was of assistance in the process of assimilation of Egyptian metrical construction, which maintained its influence up to its transformation in the fourth century B.C.

ATTIC SCULPTOR. *Head of Kouros from the Dipylon.*   *below right*
The pure and resolute forms of the great sculptor known as the Master of the Dipylon can be distinctly differentiated from the powerful, squared and balanced module created by the Master of the Kouros of Sounion. Only the damaged head remains to prove the existence of the great lost figure. The hypothesis that a magnificent damaged hand, found on the same site and now in the Athens Museum, was also part of the figure is still questionable; and the

same can be said for other fragments of a hand and a body that were found in the excavations of the Agora of Athens and attributed to the same master.

The artist accompanied the rigorous cylinder of the neck and the ovoid of the head with strongly modeled curves that concisely emphasize the essential lineaments. Other elements—such as the ears, the hair and the fillet—are developed within the terms of an austere compositional symmetry. They attain a formal unity, purified of any accidental element, in an autonomous and transcendental ideality which, in its profoundly contemplative expression, entirely fulfills those norms of beauty that for centuries were to remain among the most unalterable attributes of the Greek tradition.

BOEOTIAN ARTIST. *Head of Kouros from the Ptoion.*   *p. 81, left*
This head was part of the abundant material found in the ruins of the Temple of Apollo Ptoios of Orchomenos. The Boeotian sculptors—as can be noted in the imposing but quite different *Kouros from Orchomenos,* now also in the Athens Museum—clearly demonstrates that at the close of the seventh century they were all well acquainted with the works being produced contemporaneously in Attica and that they appropriated each other's constructional modules, techniques and morphologies. This head proves admirably how a formalistic figurative model, widely diffused and generally accepted, can be individualized with extraordinary expressive power and originality. The thin tightly closed lips, the strongly arched and sharply diverging eyebrows over the almond-shaped eyes as well as the irregularly syncopated curls bestow an individuality on this portrait that is characterized by a vital impetuosity. Its power is also conveyed by the chromatic factor, which is particularly evident in the still preserved color of the staring eyes.

ATTIC SCULPTOR. *Kouros from Anavyssos.*   *p. 83*
The inscription on the base, which many experts recognize as unquestionably part of this kouros, reads: "Stand and mourn by the grave of Kroisos, whom violent Ares snatched up from among the warriors in the front line." It is believed that this is a reference to the battle of Pallene (ca. 541–539), and the slain warrior has been identified as one of the Ionic allies that Lygdamis sent to Naxos to help Pisistratos. But the date cannot be accepted as conclusive, in view of the relationship that the statue has with certain elements of stylization of the seventh and early sixth centuries. The hypothesis that this kouros was indeed a commemorative monument to a hero of the *polis* could resolve the doubts about the original function of these virile nudes. They were neither divinities nor offerings; they were deceased defenders of the community, portrayed as terrestrial human beings.

This personage is endowed with grandeur in a highly idealized image, but his individuality is rendered by the powerfully athletic structure. Although recent theory has tended to fix the date of its composition as late as 525 B.C., its imposing stability, its radically frontal positioning, the proportions analogous to those of more primitive kouroi, and the strong adherence to Egyptian models, lead us to date it from the beginning of the sixth century.

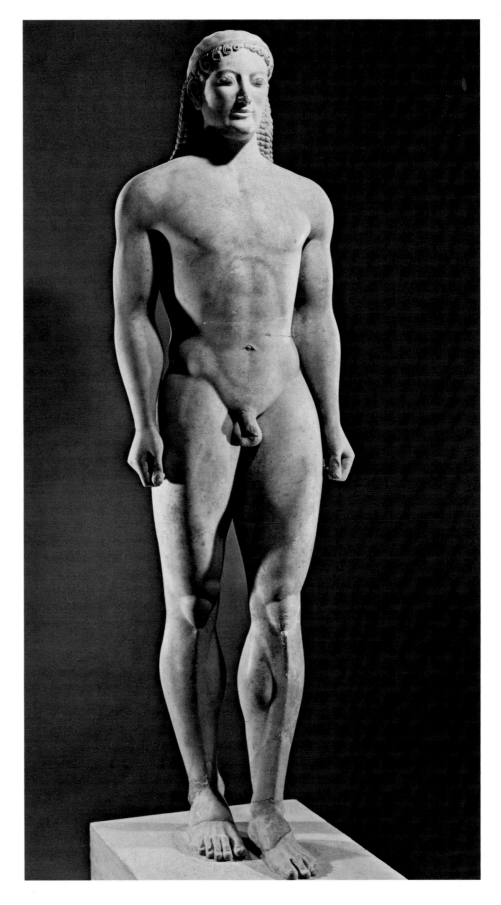

ATTIC SCULPTOR
Kouros from Anavyssos
Sixth century B.C.
Height 77".
From Anavyssos. (3851)

83

CYCLADIC SCULPTOR. *Head of Kouros from Thera.*   *p. 85*
This head, whether seen frontally or in profile as it emerges from the cylindrical mass of cascading locks and from the upper cap of spiral curls and the ribbon that follows the line of the ear, typifies the geometric structure underlying the plastic composition. The triangular and pentagonal lines which meet in parallel zones, as well as the reliefs and masses contained within curvilinear planes are conditioned by the contractions and dilations of the anatomy animated by the smile.

Many experts date this sculpture 600 B.C., but it seems more certainly the work of a sculptor who was active in the middle of the sixth century.

CYCLADIC SCULPTOR
Head of Kouros from Thera
Sixth century B.C.
Marble; height 12¼".
From Thera. (8)

CYCLADIC SCULPTOR. *Kouros from Melos.*   *p. 86*
There is a general tendency today to date a splendid series of male nudes in the Athens Museum around the middle of the sixth century or even later, although some experts still revert to the end of the preceding century or, at least, not after 590 B.C. This Kouros found in Melos repeats the general characteristics of seventh-century sculpture: identical frontal vision; the same poise of the feet and legs; the same angulation of arms and legs; identical spiral headdress that encloses the face. In view of strong variations in form, this Kouros can be sharply differentiated from the preceding sculptures of its type, and considered closer to the *Kouros from Tenea* (now in Munich), which has substantially the same proportions. When compared with the preceding kouroi, the sculptors of these last two figures evidently moved away from the geometric framework and the cubic stereometry toward curvilinear structures and molded limbs which, together with a different modular rhythm, conferred on their statues an elastic lightness and greater movement.

ATTIC SCULPTOR. *Head of Athlete with Disk.*   *p. 87*
This fragment of a grave stele was found near the so-called Wall of Themistocles in Athens. It has been suggested by several experts that another fragment in the Athens Museum (no. 83) is in fact the lower part of the same stele.

The hand of the athlete (only the thumb and palm are visible) raises the disk—on which there are still traces of blue—in such a way that the perfect circle looks like a halo around the profile in relief, bringing out the softly luminous modeling in the face of the commemorated discobolus.

Placed rigorously in the center and counterbalanced by the large braid protruding on the left—identical with the mass of locks of the so-called *Goddess of the Pomegranate* in Berlin—the face is constructed and modeled with stylistic criteria analogous to those of the *Head of Kouros* from Thera (p. 85), but with greater sensitivity.

Considered one of the most intensely creative documents of archaic Greek sculpture, this brilliant relief was the work of an Athenian master who was actively employed in the middle of the sixth century for the cemetery of the Kerameikos. He belonged to a school that was to lead to the formation of the group of sculptors responsible for the bas-reliefs of *Scenes of a Palaestra* on the base of a kouros found in Athens (p. 105).

The presence of artists from Ionia and the adjacent islands in Athens in the middle of the sixth century is well established. They have often been considered responsible for the "rebirth" of Attic art; but the latter can easily justify its own autonomous development without hypothesizing external stimuli. The sculpture that came out of Ionia was mannered and superficially cadenced, whereas the genuine Attic spirit developed greater depth, with both a more elevated tone and a more organic structure.

P. 86
CYCLADIC SCULPTOR
Kouros from Melos
Sixth century B.C.
Height 84".
From Melos. (1558)

P. 87
ATTIC SCULPTOR
Head of Athlete with Disk
Sixth century B.C.
Fragment; height 13⅜".
From Athens. (38)

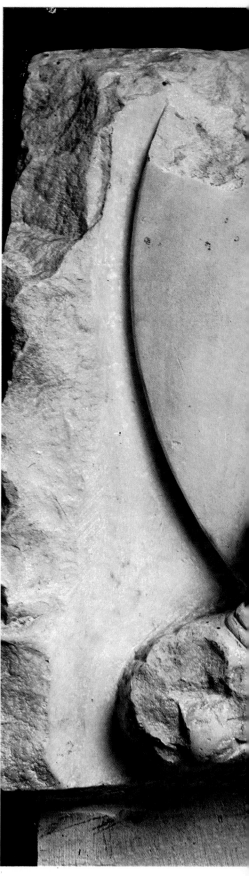

ATTIC SCULPTOR. *Kouros from Volomandra.*   *p. 89*

The particular beauty of this remarkable sculpture by a great Attic master has been ascribed to the special feeling for elegance of the Ionians. The general form corresponds to a module based on a height of 68¼", but this was employed with a flexibility of scale and with variations of iconometric norms—slight lengthenings, dilations and contractions, modifications of the relationships, softer plastic modeling—with the result that all the canonic measurements, when compared with the fundamental modules, admittedly have a far greater elasticity. It is a further development in the process of animation observed in the preceding Kouros from Melos (p. 86).

ATTIC POTTER. *Amphora with Deer.*   *p. 90*

This amphora with its perfect ovoid body (formerly believed to date from the seventh century) was painted entirely black, leaving a single panel of clear background, which is like an open window, where only one figure appears. This represents a conscious reaction to the large figurations extending even beyond the limits of the field of decoration, which had been one of the characteristics of pre-Attic pottery.

The deer is drawn with masterly elegance and in such a way as to follow the trapezoidal outline of the open space within which the subtle play of the thin legs and the branched antlers is developed. The subject of the deer represents a revival in the sixth century of an iconographic motif that was current in ancient Cretan-Mycenaean prototypes. The emphasis on the central figure is heightened by the almost total lack of decorative elements, which are replaced by wide black bands and areas, with the sole exception of the linked ornamental motif on the neck and the lance-heads rising from the base. The body of the deer was silhouetted against the background with a rapid and energetic brushstroke, reinforced by an extremely flexible graffito.

NEARCHOS. *Cantharus with Achilles Preparing for Battle,* fragment.   *p. 91*

This cantharus—a type of drinking vessel with two high handles—came to light on the Athenian Acropolis. It is signed by the ceramist Nearchos, who was active a few decades after the very different Sophilos (see p. 92).

Although this vase has suffered with time, we can still note in the color the rare employment of white—even in the upper decorative band—a contrasting background for the magnificent figures, subtly executed but conceived with monumental simplicity. The ample forms of the protagonists—men and horses painted against the bare background—are animated only by the careful lettering of the identifying inscriptions. The concentrated rhythm of the reins is remarkable, with sharp lines drawn to the maximum limit of regularity and power and directly contrasted wtih the thick manes of the animals. Inspired by the tradition of the pottery of the seventh century and particularly, it is believed, by the Nessos painter (pp. 78–79), this precious fragment is eloquent testimony of the art of another exceptional personality of the world of sixth-century Attic vase painting. It should be noted, however, that with rare exceptions, the

ATTIC SCULPTOR
Kouros from Volomandra
Sixth century B.C.
Height 70½″.
(1906)

P. 90
ATTIC POTTER
Amphora with Deer
Sixth century B.C.
Terracotta; height 13″.
(1080)

P. 91
NEARCHOS
*Cantharus with Achilles Preparing
for Battle*, fragment
Sixth century B.C.
Terracotta; height 5⅞″.
From Athens. (611)

National Museum does not offer such abundant proof of the flourishing state of the art of pottery in that period as it does for later centuries and other forms of artistic expression. Yet even if it can be verified solely by fragments, the personal language of innovators like Nearchos and Sophilos serves as both an enrichment and a clarification for a historical reconstruction of the art of vase painting in the first half of the sixth century B.C.

SOPHILOS. *Fragment of Krater with Funerary Games*
Honoring Patroclos. p. 92

This is one of three known works signed by Sophilos, an Attic painter active about 580 B.C., noted for a rare vivacity in his use of color. This fragment was found at Pharsalos in Thessaly.

Along with their return to a more ancient and disciplined tradition, the potters in the first decades of the sixth century were influenced by the coeval ceramics of Corinth, which were both decorative and imaginatively experimental. In this fragment, the four horses—one of which is all white—are launched on

SOPHILOS
Fragment of Krater with Funeral Games
Honoring Patroclos
Sixth century B.C.
Terracotta; height 3⅛".
From Pharsalos. (15499)

an exciting race and the grandstand of the stadium is crowded with tiny figures that are thoroughly aroused by sporting enthusiasm. The inspiration derived from participation in everyday life, which is not very different from our own, emphasizes the irrepressible naturalness of this singular artist. It is customary to attribute to him the reduction and transposition of the monumental and exuberant mural painting (of which nothing survives) into the limited dimensions imposed by pottery. On the basis of another signed fragment (from the Athenian Acropolis, Museum no. 587), on which were rigorously copied certain figures of the wedding procession of Tethys and Peleos of the famous Vase François, it is now generally believed that Sophilos was a predecessor of Kleitias, the great master and creator of the last-named masterpiece now on display in Florence.

CORINTHIAN PAINTER. *Small Votive Tablet with*
Procession and Sacrifice.   *below*
Discovered in the sacred grotto dedicated to the nymph of Pitsa near Corinth, this is one of the rare examples of "Archaic" Greek painting; it can be dated about 540 B.C. It represents a short procession of donors approaching a low, bare altar at the right. Offerings are being brought by garlanded women and youths: wine by the imperious woman leading the group; a lamb by the boy behind her; flowering branches by the serene figures behind a pair of musicians. It is the best preserved of four tablets found in Pitsa, which constitute, together with the *pinakes* of Pendeskoupni (now in Berlin), the most ancient documents of that painting which historians assure us was born in Corinth. Proof can be found in the analogous quality of the vase painting, in a similar employment of judicious, yet joyful, dramatic variations that do not disturb the outlines or the compositional cadences. The name of the artist was inserted in the writing at the top, but today this is unfortunately lost. All that remains is the eponym "Corinthian,"

Below
CORINTHIAN ARTIST
Small Votive Tablet with Procession and
Sacrifice
Sixth century B.C.
Tempera on wood; height 12¼".
From Pitsa. (16464)

which is, nevertheless, useful information. The small painted tablets called *pinakes* were suspended on the walls of little chapel-like structures built over tombs.

SPARTAN ARTIST. *Mirror with Figure of a Woman and Sphinxes.*   *p. 95*
As in other similar examples, this female figure wrapped in her peplos can be associated with the cult of Aphrodite, as we find her in her temple on the Acropolis of Corinth.

The slender body, only slightly veiled by the dress, is enlarged in the upper part in an elegant interplay of symmetrical and carefully balanced ornamentation. The folds of the veil, the wings of the sphinxes, the grooves of the supporting bars are all united in an expansion of rhythms and lines of force that lead upward to the attached superimposed disk, a round shining mirror. It has been felt that this was the work of an artist of the Spartan tradition, in view of the delicacy and vigor, the sharp and vibrant contour of this woman—a goddess, as indicated by the symbolism of the lion at her feet. Yet it could have been the product of a Corinthian workshop of a few decades later. This beautiful example demonstrates how articles designed for wide distribution bear the clear imprint of original and masterful creations, conferring a high esthetic quality even on objects of daily use.

ATTIC SCULPTOR. *Bas-relief with Running Hoplite.*   *p. 96, left*
This sculpture, once part of the facing of a tomb, was discovered in Athens near the Temple of Ephesos and is the work of an Athenian sculptor. It is generally dated around 520 B.C., but perhaps it should be placed nearer the middle of the century. It is popularly known as the "Stele of the Warrior of Marathon," because of the obvious parallel between the figure of the athlete driven to the pangs of exhaustion and the dramatic arrival of the famous heroic messenger. But the dating certainly excludes any such relationship.

The Attic artist saw his figure from three different visual angles: the head with the large helmet in profile toward the left and enclosed in a semicircle; the chest and the bent arms frontally, and therefore excluded from the circle, moving in the opposite direction from the profile; the legs rotating in their running or final leaping movement, in accordance with a formula that was frequently found in figurations of gorgons and possessing the same periodic valence as the Ionic volutes crowning the top of the stele like a capital. The simultaneous presence of frontal and profile poses is often found in Hellenic sculpture and painted pottery of the seventh century and could have been derived from either the Cretan or the Egyptian tradition. The employment of simple or double torsion was widespread in the first half of the sixth century—Corfu, Selinunte, Delphi, etc.—and in Athens this had an exceptional model in the Hekatompedon toward the end of the century.

Whether this is the depiction of a race or of a step in a war dance, the hoplite—who in his kinetic movement involves parallel curvatures of the arms and legs and the spinning torsion of the body—is one of the most creatively formal visions ever attained in sublimating a daily event.

11691

SCULPTOR OF THESSALY. *Young Girl Running.* *below, right*

This sculpture was found in Dodona, Thessaly, where at the end of the sixth century and the beginning of the fifth there appears to have been a vast production of bronzes, which indicates how widespread was the diffusion of Peloponnesian art, even in the remote areas of northern Greece. This piece is part of the Karapanos Collection, which contains the important finds from the excavations made in the Epeiros region between 1875 and 1877. A maiden with short locks and long braids is portrayed running, which serves to confirm the feminine presence in the Olympic games, as related in the detailed description of Pausanias.

The conventional scheme is still the polygonal structure established by the archaic artists: the figure is enclosed in a rectangle; the arms and the upper part of the legs are seen frontally; the lower part of the legs is in profile, which imposed a torsion of the bust and a diagonal angulation of the head, which is therefore seen in half-profile. The composition, in other words, is based on the virtual polyhedral rotation so common in sixth century art which was to continue

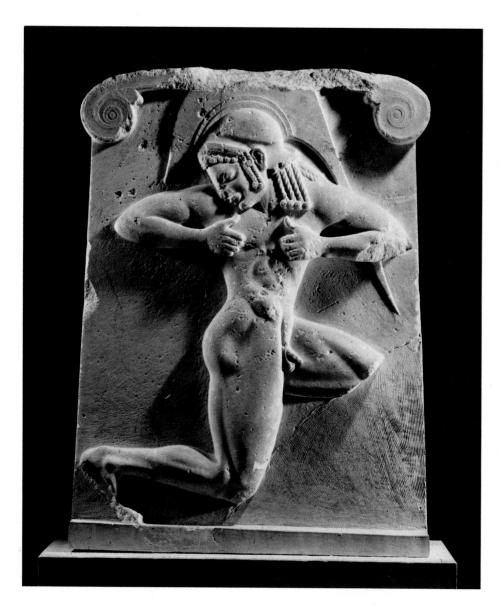

Left
ATTIC SCULPTOR
Bas-relief with Running Hoplite
Sixth century B.C.
Marble; height 40".
From Athens. (1959)

Below
SCULPTOR OF THESSALY
Young Girl Running
Sixth century B.C.
Bronze; height 48¾".
From Dodona. (24)

BOEOTIAN SCULPTOR
Stele of Alxenor
Ca. 500 B.C.
Marble; height 80¾".
From Orchomenos. (39)

97

during later centuries, especially in the design of coins. This perfectly preserved statuette has been dated in various decades: 540, 530, 510, 500 B.C.

BOEOTIAN SCULPTOR. *Stele of Alxenor.*   *p. 97*
In this stele inscribed "Alxenor the Naxian made me. Admire me," the long rectangle is completely filled by the figure of a man offering a locust to his dog. It was discovered at Orchomenos in Boeotia and is believed to be the work of a local sculptor; many experts maintain that it was executed at the turn of the sixth-fifth centuries, or even as late as 490 B.C.

This bas-relief is an example of a strophic composition that later was to have a widespread influence on Attic art. With the elongated vertical of the stele and the visual direction clearly indicated by the staff pointing upward, the artist realized an explicit sinusoidal cadence by curving the figure from the head to the feet along the arm and the jumping dog. An essential undulation characterizes all the rhythms, particularly in the drapery which, from the circle on the shoulder, is amplified lower down in a series of centrifugal and diverging curves. The rhythms are emphasized by the sculptural form itself, which juts out only slightly and is grooved by subtle graphic lines which appear even on the bare, veined arm and on the expressive profile of the face.

In this case again a daily domestic subject was the basis for a composition offering limitless opportunities for repetition. A stele portraying the same subject, dating from the beginning of the fifth century and found in Apollonia (now in the Museum of Sofia), presents a variation on the mode.

Right and detail p. 99
ARISTOKLES OF ATHENS
Sepulchral Stele of Aristion
Ca. 520 B.C.
Height 94⅜".
From Velanidezza. (29)

ARISTOKLES OF ATHENS. *Sepulchral Stele of Aristion.   right, detail p. 99*
This work was signed by Aristokles, one of several names of sculptors of the Archaic epoch which have fortunately come down to us. It is a commemorative stele found in Attica, portraying the soldier Aristion as a typical warrior of the period of the Persian wars. As is generally the case with most of the surviving steles, it shows a single figure occupying the entire lengthened rectangular field that contains it; and there is a total correspondence between space and figure in the compositional equilibrium.

The original painted decoration, of which a few traces are still visible, contributed to giving the hollowed and engraved, but barely jutting relief a scaled superimposition of planes and depth, for instance between the two legs and the flat arm in the foreground. The folds of the drapery, on the other hand, are only sketchily indicated with shallow, angular incisions.

The reduction of the profile and the use of color have frequently raised the hypothesis of a relationship with contemporary potters of the end of the sixth century, such as Sosias, Peithrinos.

BOEOTIAN SCULPTOR. *Kouros from the Ptoion.*　　　　*below, left*
Clearly evident is the contrast between the radiant plasticity of the breathing youthful body and the engraved decorative graphics of the head, which was added to the headless torso at a relatively recent date. The head is also presumed to be of Boeotian origin, but it was the work of an artisan who was still following the sculptural formulas and solutions of the early years of the century. It differs considerably, therefore, from the fluent harmony of the body which, together with the *Apollo* found in the same Theban temple and the *Kouros of Aristodikos* (p. 101), is a significant example of that transformation of the male nude during the last decades of the sixth century that was to result in the audacious equilibrium and pulsating vitality of the Kouroi and Apollos from Melos, Volomandra, etc.

Lower left
BOEOTIAN SCULPTOR
Kouros from the Ptoion
Ca. 520 B.C.
Height 37⅜".
(12)

BOEOTIAN SCULPTOR. *Kouros (Apollo?) from the Ptoion.*　　*below, right*
A dedicatory inscription to the god of the silver bow found in the ruins of the Temple of Apollo Ptoios near Thebes has strengthened the hypothesis that this mutilated statue, offered by two devotees—Pythias and Aiskrion—is a portrait

Lower right
BOEOTIAN SCULPTOR
Kouros from the Ptoion (Apollo?)
Ca. 510 B.C.
Marble; 40½".
(20)

ATTIC SCULPTOR
Kouros of Aristodikos
Ca. 500 B.C.
Height 76¾".
From Anavyssos. (3938)

of the god himself. The loss of the arms and legs emphasizes in a certain way the powerful impression of the harmonious structure, all light or tenuous shadows flowing fluidly over the modeled planes in continuous waves out of which rises the head shaped with delicate elegance. The face is framed by a rhythmically undulating crown of compact curls. The sculpture can be linked to such others as the *Strangford Kouros* in London and the *Theseus* in the Temple of Apollo in Eretria. In the development of the athletic muscular system, which replaces the isolated polygonal elements even graphically, it bears a resemblance to the *Kouros of Aristodikos* (p. 101) with which it shares the movement of the arms in a position analogous to that of a charioteer.

ATTIC SCULPTOR. *Kouros of Aristodikos.*   *p. 101*
This sculpture is in an exceptionally fine condition including the base on which is inscribed the name of the person to whom it was dedicated, Aristodikos, a name recognized as belonging to the family of the Alcmenidi.

As in some other figures of the end of the century, one notes even a vague intention of doing a portrait and an abandonment of the emotionless idealization of the preceding kouroi. The inscription, which is surely pertinent, leads us to believe that this—and perhaps other similar sculptures of the middle of the century—were originally intended for the tombs of deceased youths, as we have noted for the *Kouros of Anavyssos* (p. 83), which was found in the same place as this figure.

Given its more perfect state of preservation as compared to similar statues, the *Aristodikos* has been examined closely as regards its measurements and proportions, which are so different from those of the kouroi of the sixth century, despite the fact that for ritual reasons it retains the same slow pace. Yet through the symmetrical flexion of the arms and the softer modeling of the plastic masses, the power of the frontal and lateral positions is reduced and a generally united, continuous movement is created.

ATTIC SCULPTOR. *Apollo of Piraeus.*   *p. 103*
This bronze statue found in Piraeus in 1959, which together with a group of other sculptures appears to have been stored in preparation for shipment to Rome at the beginning of the first century A.D., is impressive.

The bronze itself with its patina strengthens the sensation of an uninterrupted formation of the plastic mass that perfectly expresses the energy and poise of a vital organism. As in the older kouroi—from Melos or Volomandra—one notes more or less obvious departures from the sculptural canons: a lowering of the overall height (5'8"); shifting of the navel; unequal length of the arms. The modifications are proof of the determining exigency: the dominion of an expansive energy that ill supports equivalence, symmetry or inertia. Despite its

ATTIC SCULPTOR
Apollo of Piraeus
Ca. 500 B.C.
Bronze; height 75⅝".
From Piraeus. (6446)

affinity with contemporary kouroi, this figure has a clearly declared ritual posture: the right hand bore a cup, while the left held a bow (and arrows?); the slightly inclined head looks down at the cup; and the short, intense forward movement of the right leg is counterbalanced by a static, refined sense of momentary equilibrium. The sculptor did not ignore the canons of geometric structure, but the volume was considered in terms of active movement; and the transient, precarious immobility was attributed solely to an instant of equilibrium of the active forces. As in architecture the term "function"—later called "strength"—is used, so in a sculpture such as the *Apollo of Piraeus* the substratum of the potential relationship of forces is clear. A great transformation was taking place and we shall see its effects later on: the passage from a situation dominated by a geometric compositional concept and a progressive succession of single structures to a congruence based on the integration of the internal dynamics.

ATTIC SCULPTOR. *Dog and Cat Fight Restrained by Two Seated Youths, with Two Onlookers; Ball Players; Runner at Starting Point, Two Wrestlers, Javelin Thrower.* *p. 105–107*

These three bas-reliefs decorated the base of a kouros statue found among the ruins of the so-called Wall of Themistocles, which was hurriedly constructed around Athens, even using fragments of works of art, as protection against a threatened attack of the Persians in 479–478 B.C. Brought to light in the same place were three other bas-reliefs of an analogous base (no. 3477) with different athletic scenes (*Chariot Race, "Hockey" Players*) employing a similar, but considerably impoverished, plastic language. These can be dated several decades later. Since the ones illustrated here can be attributed to the last years of the sixth century, they reveal the extent to which athletics pursued in the palaestrae at the time of Pisistratos and Cleisthenes were considered to be complementary to the practice of art.

The bas-reliefs shown here were cut with a uniform background and bear traces of the red paint that covered them: a fact that underlines the affinity of these reliefs with contemporary vase painting, particularly that of Euthymides, from whom were derived the characteristic folds and the undulating pace, or of Euphronius, in whose work we find the same attention to anatomy analytically enhanced in the energy and power of movement.

Historically the Greek athletic system—and before that, the Egyptian—was based on geometry. The conventions of the use of arms and of fencing were fundamentally geometric norms: a metrical content of Greek culture that existed likewise in its poetry, music, art, science and exercise. Anatomy was not dissection but research into the functional capacities of the body, which are increased and perfected the more the body is educated by exercise and by the personification of geometry. Its categorically harmonious characteristics are found in gymnastic games, dance and wrestling. Human bodies, singly or engaged in multiple or collective operations, constitute in and of themselves the figures and the essential transformations of geometry by which they are reciprocally imbued. We learn from Vitruvius that the *"quadratio"* of the rhythm component of the cosmos is revealed in the articulation of the body, in the perfectly integrated figures of the circle and the square. The compositions and the situations of these gymnastic reliefs are subject to the geometry which these disciplined bodies themselves build. The celebration of this correspondence, which was so vivid in the minds and feelings of the Greeks, is evident in the forms and the special subjects of these reliefs, which in themselves condense several fundamental aspects of Greek life and civilization.

P. 105 upper panel
ATTIC SCULPTOR
Dog and Cat Fight Restrained by Two Seated Youths; Two Onlookers
Ca. 500 B.C.
Height 12¼"; width 26½".
From Athens. (3476)

P. 105, center panel
ATTIC SCULPTOR
Ball Players
Ca. 500 B.C.
Height 12¼"; width 26½".
From Athens. (3476)

P. 105, lower panel and detail pp. 106–107
ATTIC SCULPTOR
Runner at the Starting Point, Two Wrestlers, Javelin Thrower
Ca. 500 B.C.
Height 12¼"; width 26 ½".
From Athens. (3476)

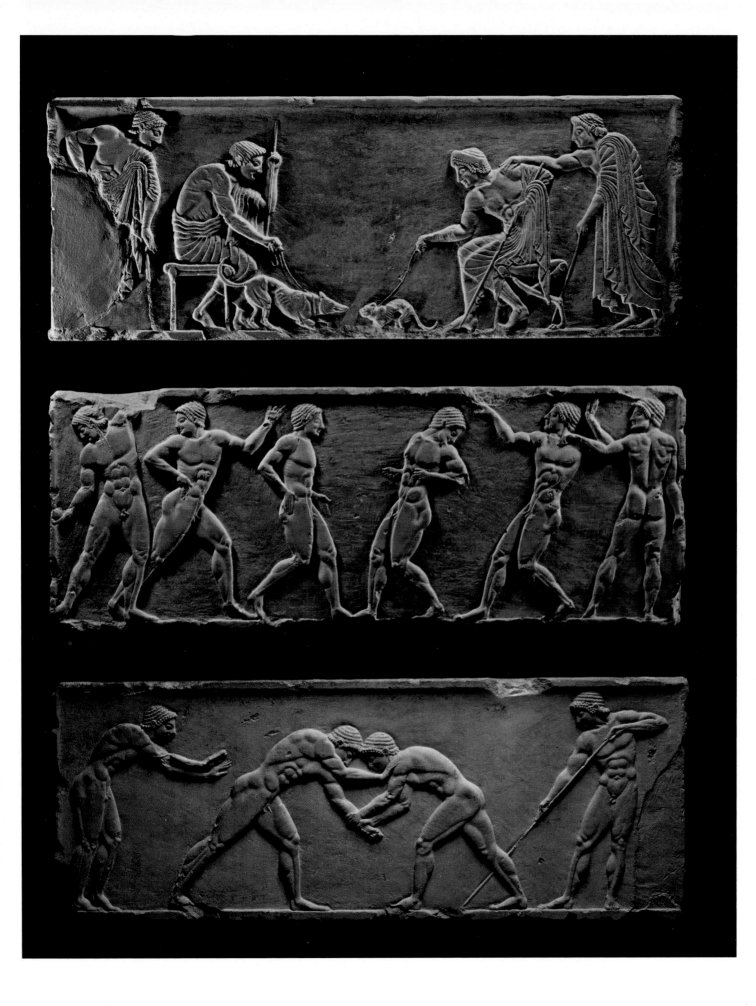

ATTIC SCULPTOR. *Head of a Kore (Maiden).*   *p. 109, left*
The external formulas of this head from Eleusis—above all the characteristic solution of the headdress with its heavy mass of uniform and parallel, wavy braids combed low on the forehead—return to famous models of antiquity such as the *Head of Athena* from the west pediment of the Temple of Athena Aphaia in Aegina, which is preserved today, together with a conspicuous group of surviving fragments, in the Antikensammlung of Munich (even if polished and neoclassicized by Thorwaldsen). Then there are the heads of warriors (nos. 1933–1938, Athens Museum) which are the remains of the first version of the east pediment and contemporaneous with the construction of the temple—ca. 510 B.C.; that pediment was replaced by another in 490 B.C. which also depicted battle scenes of the Trojan War.

Unquestionably contemporary with the latter, and with analogous korai from the Athenian Acropolis, this splendid head can also be dated from the same years of the fifth century. There is a difference, however, because added to the fleshy feminine faces of the so-called "severe sculpture" there is an unusual search for the transparent values of light and shade in the delicate and silken modeling which, exploiting the luminosity of the marble, renders this Kore sensitive and refined, giving it an accent of dreamy, tender introspection.

KRITIOS (?). *Head of an Ephebos.*   *p. 109, right*
This handsome bronze found on the Athenian Acropolis has justifiably been associated with the *Kouros* of the same origin (no. 698, Acropolis Museum) which some experts believe to be a work of the great sculptor Kritios. He was the author of, among other sculptures, the famous group of *The Tyrannicides* (477–476 B.C.) which we know unfortunately solely through mutilated marble copies in Naples, Rome and New York.

The small head is a priceless document of the moment of intense research in sculptural form that characterized the Athenian Kritios and his Ionic associate Nesiotes. But there were also other masters, such as the author of the *Blond Ephebos,* active in the two decades from 480 to 460 B.C. The facial structure already noted in the statuary group surrounding the *Aristodikos* (p. 101) now assumes a different character. The heads of the sixth-century kouroi were based on curvilinear rhythms of both design and volume that required arched eyebrows and the animated semblance of a smile which, in turn, give an oblique slant to the eyes. Here the head, retaining the limpid spherical, ovoidal, cylindrical form, is characterized, under the crown of hair, by conspicuous horizontal rhythms that exclude the mimetic contractions, and construct the facial form in a series of rhythmically modeled curves which are in opposition to the vertical of the straight nose. It is a structural composition which creates a steady chiaroscuro on the austerely contained volume. The general effect is one of simple and substantiated concision, which has encouraged the scholars to speak of a "severe style" for works like this attributable to the hand of Kritios.

Employing a commonly known technique, eyes of vitreous paste were inserted into the bronze giving the statue the character of a living presence like that which could be obtained with paint, although it certainly was not realistic. When observing ancient sculpture we must remember that the habit of considering it achromatic and marblelike is historical and had its origins in the fifteenth century when the first unpainted—or, at least, devoid of color as a result of long periods under ground or other damage—Roman copies came to light. From the Humanistic age to the Neoclassical period, sculptural form and its relative chiaroscuro were considered to be the supreme values of art as compared to color, which was considered as purely accidental if not hedonistic. From that prejudice was born the habit, still tenaciously held today, to assume that all Greek sculpture was colorless with a partial exclusion of artistic values. Yet the plastic arts of Greece still have to be studied systematically if we want to be precise as to when and why statuary was colored or painted monochromatically to resemble pottery. When the artists applied color or, as in this case, employed the vitreous glaze for the eyes, they intended to create between the work of art and the observer a relationship of basic unity resting not only on the differences of dimension and the absence of mobility but also on a fictitious naturalness, chosen and adopted on the basis of its customary communicative value and recognized as such, for example, the glance of an eye.

It is important to remember that figurative and imitative sculpture, even if idealized, was defined by Plato (427–347 B.C.) as "unchaste" and inferior. The philosopher contrasted it with "fantastic" art, i.e., an art of abstract forms created by the pure mind, and with "perspective" art, i.e., the attempt to reproduce the rational structure of reality—not its contingent and physical appearance.

COPY FROM AN ATHENIAN SCULPTOR OF THE
FIFTH CENTURY B.C. (KALAMIS?). *Apollo of the Omphalos.*   *p. 111*
This splendid marble copy—which some experts attribute to the Roman
period—of a famous bronze original was found in the Theater of Dionysos in
Athens near a symbol of an *omphalos* (the conical symbol of Apollo), from
which it derives its distinguishing name.

It has been linked to various masters who are known to have been active in
Attica toward the end of the first half of the fifth century on the basis of
descriptions of works and styles that have been transmitted to us by the
historians. The name of Myron is often mentioned, but also especially that of
Pythagoras of Samos with a proposal to identify it with one of his sculptures,
Euthymos the Boxer, quite certainly executed in 472 B.C. Pythagoras was
certainly one of the major figures in the sculpture of the time, displaying an
"advanced naturalism" (Pliny) and a "new sense of composition," inasmuch as
he "aimed primarily at rhythm and symmetry" (Diogenes Laertios). Even more
convincing is the widely held proposal to recognize in this work the *Apollo
Alexikakos* of a slightly younger sculptor, the Athenian Kalamis, whom both
Quintilian and Cicero insisted was still attached to the tradition of archaic forms
but with a refinement of execution and a grandeur of conception that made him
"one of the excellent artists of his time."

If we can suppose that the author of this extraordinary copy had the
sensitivity of a Pheidias—thus giving particular importance to the back of the
statue and to the rhombus of tension in the torso, endowing it with a pulsating
energy (less noticeable in the front of the statue, where the play of the
equilibrium is predominant)—then we can draw the conclusion that the
innovation of Kritios, as compared, for example, to the author of the *Apollo of
Piraeus* (p. 103), lies in the fact that he opened a new period of research both in
Olympia—the *Oinomaos* of the east pediment of the Temple of Zeus—and in
Athens. Already in the first half of the fifth century this innovating tactic had
achieved definite results in the dactylic rhythm developed on a sinuous
self-rotating axis. We are justified, therefore, in seeing in the *Apollo of the
Omphalos* the solution of the *Doryphoros* that embodied the great "canon" of
Polykleitos.

ATTIC SCULPTOR (KALAMIS?). *Bronze Divinity from Cape
Artemision.*   *pp. 112–113*
Many critics have linked this splendid sculpture of the middle of the fifth century
to the "simple and disciplined" art of Kalamis, who was born in Boeotia but
became completely merged into the artistic environment of Attica. In the
absence of identifying attributes such as a three-pronged spear or a bolt of
lightning, the work has been variously interpreted as an image of Poseidon or,
according to more recent opinion, of Zeus.

The search for monumentality, which is emphasized by the colossal
dimensions, is admirably realized in the ample gesture of the horizontal arms, in
the calm stance with the powerful spread of the legs, in the splendid volumetric
structure of the large body moving forward with grandiose impetus while yet
retaining a poise of perfect equilibrium.

The unquestionable resemblance to the *Apollo of the Omphalos* (p. 111),
especially if we imagine the original of the latter in bronze, has led many
students to the conclusion that they were the works of one and the same master.
This statue was found at Cape Artemision and clearly reveals similarities with
the metopes of Temple "E" of Selinunte (note the one with Zeus and Hera)
which, in turn, confirms its dating.

The figure was unquestionably derived, as far as the general distributive
system of its triangular components is concerned, from the initial figures of *The*

COPY FROM AN ATHENIAN SCULPTOR
OF THE FIFTH CENTURY (KALAMIS?)
Apollo of the Omphalos
Fifth century B.C.
Marble; height 70¼".
From Athens. (45)

P. 112, detail P. 113
ATTIC SCULPTOR (KALAMIS ?)
Bronze Divinity from Cape Artemision
Fifth century B.C.
Bronze; height 82¼".
From Cape Artemision. (15161)

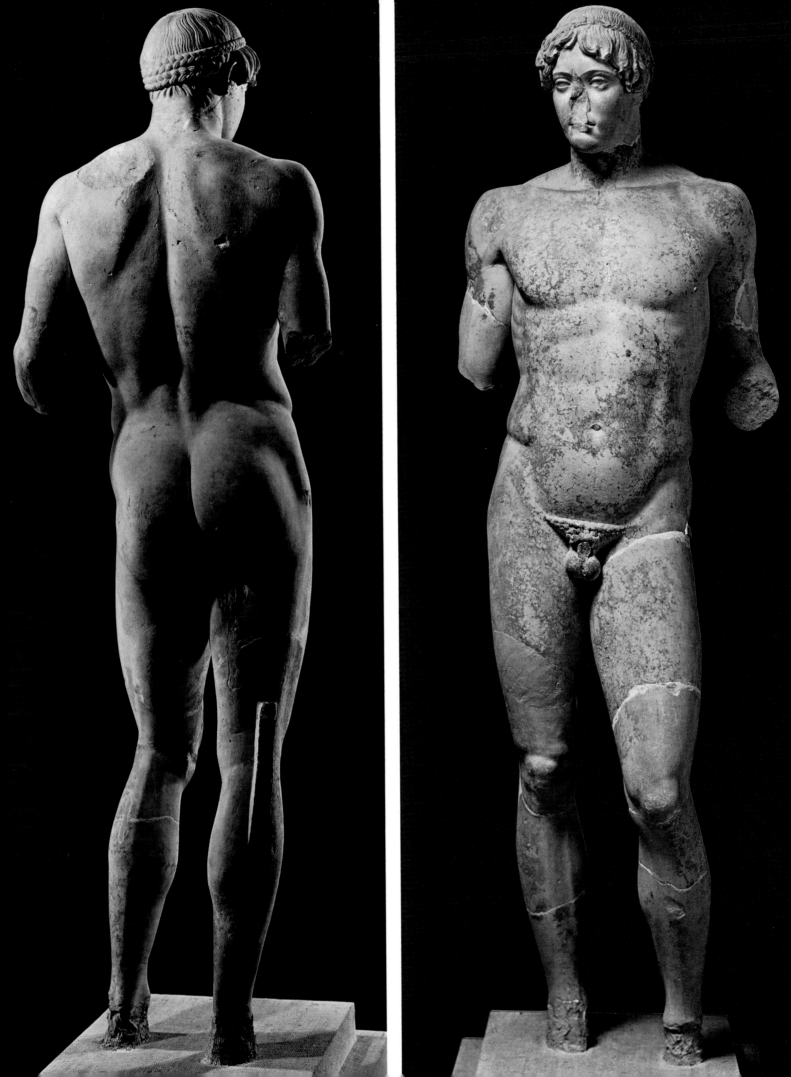

Tyrannicides of Kritios, which, at the same time, represented a new composition of the more ancient motifs of the single step and the pace. A double angle of vision prevails—frontal and profile—but it is not without intermediary articulations created by the torsion of the head and body. Poised in the moment of throwing the trident or the lightning bolt (held by the raised right arm), the figure is constructed from the thorax to the tense right leg on a curved axis resembling a taut bow that introduces a factor of restrained impulse into the equilibrium of the angulations. The skillful construction of the figure, often adopted as a model of canonic instruction, gives the statue a detached superhuman majesty.

BOEOTIAN SCULPTOR. *Stele of a Youth with Dog.*   lower right
Found in Thespia and datable around the middle of the fifth century B.C., this work follows closely the archaic module of the rectangular form. The stele is entirely given over to the image of a deceased youth, inserted into a niche framed by pilasters and surmounted by a small triangular pediment. The figuration takes up once again a theme that was quite common in the last decades of the sixth century *(Stele of Alxenor,* p. 97). The unknown youth who, in this high relief is a perfect example of the application of Polykleitos' canon of equilibrium, is realized in a two-dimensional projection: the sinusoidal curve is constructed in counterbalancing semicircles and quarters of a circle, thus emphasizing the harmoniously outlined pose of the figure.

ATTIC SCULPTOR. *Stele of Demokleides.*   p. 115
This rectangular tablet of reduced dimensions is a modest memorial to a lost sailor, Demokleides, who is sitting grieving on the prow of the ship that will never bring him back. The helmet and the shield on the right and the rudderless helm indicating the destruction of the ship are the only meager elements that, together with the figure, interrupt the vast background of the relief, which was originally painted blue like the sea on which the deceased warrior's ship was sailing. It is less certain, but probable, that the boat too, although now only a bare outline, was tinged with one color or another. This is not a masterpiece but, rather, an article of a production that was directed toward a wide public; and it is for that reason that the intensity of evocation and emotional suggestion emerge all the more strongly, because the firm and concise form is fixed in a synthetic and irreplaceable image. The theme with its simple profiles and planes was to be taken up repeatedly for a long time. The level of achievement of Greek sculpture of the fifth century can be judged by the originality and variety of these widespread manifestations.

ATTIC ARTIST. *Funerary Vase with two Warriors and a Horseman; a Woman and a Maid.*   p. 116
This marble vase can be dated about 440 B.C., recalling the famous *Stele of Mynnion* (no. 763 of the Athens Museum) which is likewise Athenian and almost contemporary with the resplendent moment of Pheidias' creations for the Parthenon. On the empty spaces of the vase, between a figuration of inferior quality (leave-taking of two hoplites), another artist inserted the completely independent group of the woman with her servant in very shallow relief, engraved as if by a chisel at varying depths. The outlines of the figures and particularly the development of the folds of the dress glide over the background

114

P. 115
ATTIC SCULPTOR
Stele of Demokleides
Second half fifth century
Height 27½".
(752)

Below
BOEOTIAN SCULPTOR
Stele of a Youth with Dog
Ca. 540 B.C.
Calcareous stone; height 68⅞".
From Thespiae. (937)

ΔΗΜΟΚΛΕΙΔΗΣ : ΔΗΜΗΤΡΙΟ

recording even the slightest mutation of light and shade with an effect identical to that of a charcoal drawing. It is evident, in view of the rare state of preservation of this unusual work, how, after imposing a first and precise outline, the artist accurately and lovingly elaborated and refined this little masterpiece. In sharp contrast with the banality of the original decoration of the vase, the addition was enhanced by its imaginative, rapid and concentrated execution: in fact, it is incomprehensible for what reason or caprice it was inserted on an object that was complete in and of itself. If so little notice of it is taken today, it must have been totally overlooked at the time of its creation, when the color that originally covered the entire body of the vase made it impossible or, at least, extremely difficult to be seen at all.

ATTIC SCULPTOR. *Demeter and Persephone with Triptolemos.*   *p. 117*
Originally this votive relief was colored, and ears of wheat being handed to the youth by Demeter and a crown being placed on his head by Persephone were of metal, probably gold. It was found in the Telesterion of Eleusis which was destroyed by the Persians in 480 B.C. but immediately reconstructed, almost as an enormous showcase for this precious triad, which is considered one of the most deeply impressive creations of Greek art and by many attributed to Pheidias himself.

The "pictorial" quality of the majority of the bas-reliefs produced in the second half of the fifth century in the wake of Pheidias' teachings and influence is singularly evident in this superb group of figures which emerge delicately and almost as if drawn on the smooth background by the carving which inscribes the animated movement of the heavy, varied and splintered cadences of the peploi and mantles, in noticeable contrast to the flow of the thick, wavy hair. This bas-relief—with the arrangement of the group giving the impression of standing on a narrow stage—resolved an extraordinary challenge as regards the organization of its multiple planes, for example in the insertion of the youth between an external and an internal bar, as if he were passing through a doorway. The breathing quality of the planes with figures in profile and on the diagonal in the brief space between the foreground threshold and the background was derived directly from Pheidias and the panels of the Parthenon. The same can be said for the rivulets of light in the lively chiaroscuro that illuminates the columnar figures of Demeter and Persephone. One is led to believe that the artist calculated a lighting that would be neither from a single source nor directed; he relied on the complete daily arc of solar light, thus maintaining for the relief an ineluctable capacity to impress the observer, subtracting it from any external limitations. The universality of Pheidias' chiaroscuro, as realized in his deep-set metopes and his reliefs, was renewed here with great creative imagination.

ATTIC SCULPTOR. *Votive Relief of Xenokrateia.*   *p. 118*
This marble in deep relief came from a temple—Neon Phaleron—at the mouth of the river Kephisos, where it was found in 1783. The inscription of the supporting base states that Xenokrateia, mother of Xemades, founded the temple and dedicated it to the river and to the gods honored on its altar; a surviving stone reveals the names of the latter and the votive relief portrays them. The three smaller figures are the donor and her child listening to the admonitions of a priest who was evidently inspired by the semigod Kephisos, erect in profile at the center against the background. Apollo can be identified as

P. 117
ATTIC SCULPTOR
Demeter and Persephone with Triptolemos
Ca. middle fifth century B.C.
Height 86⅝".
From Eleusis. (126)

Below
ATTIC SCULPTOR
Funerary Vase with Two Warriors and a Horseman; Woman and Maid
Ca. 440 B.C.
Marble; height 26⅜".
From Athens. (835)

the figure on the tripod at far left and next to him are Artemis and, perhaps, Latona; at extreme right, the bull with the human head is the river god Achelous, accompanied by nymphs and Hestia.

The group is arranged along the elongated rectangular panel and the personages depicted have the appearance of conversing in a friendly meeting. The formal language of the sculptor does not offer any innovation but is deferential to the great and fertile Athenian school of Pheidias—particularly the workshop of the Parthenon sculptures, 445–435 B.C. Kephisos, in the center of the composition, connects the vertical and parallel figures that are linked clearly together—not without a certain overemphatic insistence—by a sequence of three large profiled triangles partly repeated in the side figures in such a way that the symmetry of the plan does not transcend the naturalness of the scene. It is a masterful work, almost a standard text, that translates and revives Pheidias' style with great nobility and beauty.

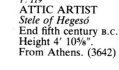

P. 119
ATTIC ARTIST
Stele of Hegesó
End fifth century B.C.
Height 4' 10⅝".
From Athens. (3642)

ATTIC SCULPTOR. *Stele of Hegeso.*   *p. 119*
Discovered in the Kerameikos of Athens, this memorial gravestone can be dated toward the end of the fifth century, although a few critics are tempted to assign a later date (390 B.C.), when Attic sculptors revived Pheidias' sculptural language. We believe that it was the work of one of the master's direct disciples. The stele assumed the architectonic style that was to remain a constant characteristic of the numerous funerary stelai of the fourth century: a niche with pilasters and pediment but expanded in comparison with the traditional examples previously known in such a way as to contain not only the single figure of the deceased but also one or more mourning persons.

From the inscription on the pediment we learn that the deceased was called Hegeso, the daughter or, perhaps, the wife of Proxemos. The lovely young woman is portrayed in the act of taking a ring from the jewel case which is

Below
ATTIC ARTIST
Votive Relief of Xenokrateia
End fifth century B.C.
Height 22".
From Neon Phaleron. (2756)

offered by her handmaid. Traces of color confirm that even in this instance the stele was completed with painted sections: the necklace and the entire (blue) background.

It is a magnificent example of the sensitivity with which the art of Pheidias on the Parthenon was understood in Athens. The drapery, because of the peculiar transparency and the subtlety of the modeling, does not hide the extraordinary softness of the forms that it covers; it even suggests and exalts them and coagulates into groups of folds that thicken as they move and drop away from the body, thus acting as factors of equilibrium and reflection.

The delicate body of the young servant, still alive and partaking of worldly existence, is intact in the standing pose that shows the long dress of a foreign style (which, because of similarities in the draping of the peplos on the figure, many critics have related to the Aphrodite of the "genetrix" type, which has survived in numerous copies). This small figure serves to emphasize the resplendent beauty of the deceased young woman in her tranquil pose, which harmonizes with the elliptic lines of the chair. The supreme composure of style and intensity of expression make this stele of Hegeso an outstanding masterpiece.

DOURIS. *Kylix with Youth Making an Offering.*   *p. 121*
Signed by the painter Douris, who was active in Athens from 500 to ca. 470 B.C., this kylix (drinking cup) portrays a subject that will be found repeatedly on numerous objects of this master's copious productions. Thirty-two signed vases as well as a large number of other works are recognized as his. The same theme is found with minimum variations of pose on the Arnheim Kylix.

As a typical example of the artist's harmonious and refined academic production, this work displays a distinguishing feature in his pictorial language: the sharp delineation of the figure against the black background, not only when, as in this case, the personage stands alone, solving by itself the compositional problem through the equilibrium conferred on the human body and the objects—plate, vase, altar—arranged with deliberation within the circle of the vessel, but also in many other figurations that are often complex but never crowded or overloaded. The artist also succeeds in obtaining a singular effect with the folds of the dress which serve to express the agile arms and legs and the lithe elegance of the stepping movement. This kylix should be considered a youthful work, dating from a time when Douris was still strongly influenced by the first masters of the red-figure.

PAN PAINTER. *Pelike with Scenes of Herakles in Egypt.*   *p. 122*
The pelike is a variation of the amphora with a more bulging body and a wider mouth. The artist, named after a scene depicted on a krater now in Boston, was active about 470 B.C. and, even though linked to the traditions of the preceding century, introduced a new, personal note into the great Attic pottery of the beginning of the fifth century. His painting, which is characterized by an impetuous and vivid manner, has many points in common with monumental sculpture. The large group on the front of this vase—constructed on repeated pyramids rising in such a way as to exploit the curvature of the vessel, ascending from its wide base to its ample mouth—is remarkably dynamic both in the animated representation of the event and, more significantly, in the composition of the figures alternately thrust upward or contracted in a downward movement. This is obtained with shifts of the sharp angles of the moving arms and legs, of the rotating objects and of the undulating folds of the draperies in an apparent vortex which, however, is magnificently restrained by the rigorous discipline of

the composition. This movement—in a synthesis which concentrates and intensifies it—is even more evident on the back of the vase with a scene of fleeing Egyptians that inscribes the diverging directions of the figures in an upright spiral movement. Sometimes classified as a "mannerist," the Pan Painter appears to us as a composer of extraordinary capacity; he succeeds in giving to his dramatic content the maximum intensity without ever losing clarity in transfiguring it into expressive and formal eurythmy.

DOURIS
Kylix with Youth Making an Offering
First half fifth century B.C.
height 3 ½"; diam. 9".
From Athens. (1666)

ERETRIA PAINTER. *Epinetron with Alkestis and Sisters on Her Wedding Day.* *below*

The painter of this work is named after the place where it was found. In the extraordinary panorama offered by vase painting in the fifth century—so abounding in works by strongly individualized personalities (for the most part singly identified), and so varied in numerous directions, even in decorative techniques and the forms of the vases—the Eritrea Painter is distinguished by a note of imaginative refinement and animated beauty in small-scale works. In this example, the gentle fantasy of young women in floating peploi lends charm to episodes filled with a profusion of ornamental elements, bunches of flowers, crowns, wreaths, magnificent fabrics, affectionate pet animals, splendidly painted amphoras and jars.

Judged by some critics as a calligraphic or "mannerist" decorator, the works of this potter nevertheless can be regarded as a fundamental document from the end of the fifth century B.C. of the transposition into the art of vase-painting of certain aspects that the historians insist were present in the great mural painting of the epoch, in particular the elegant and sophisticated aestheticism and the psychological refinements that tradition indicates can be associated with Parrhasios of Ephesos.

PAINTER OF THE BOSANQUET VASE. *Lekythos with a Young Woman Honoring the Tomb of a Hero.* *p. 125*

The lekythos is a small vase with a lengthened cylindrical body, thin neck, wide mouth and single handle, used as a funerary urn or container of perfumed essences, and decorated with tempera painting.

In the complex panorama of great painting of the second half of the fifth century, there are widely varying manifestations of different and at times

antithetical inspiration. These range from detached, even caricatural, characterizations of daily life left by Pauson to the visions of mannerist grace of the late followers of Polygnotos; and from the investigations of chiaroscuro of the great Zeuxis to the pregnant outlines of Parrhasios. It is customary to find an echo of the art of Parrhasios in the white-background lekythoi created by a group of Attic potters of the second half of the fifth century, of which the Athens Museum has an exceptional series of masterpieces. Among the personalities who have been identified is the so-called Bosanquet Painter to whom this vase—dated 440–430 B.C.—has been attributed.

On either side of a funerary monument the artist has placed two figures—one representing the deceased whose noble body is accented by the red chlamys thrown over his shoulder; the other, the trembling figure of a young woman, the angular and interrupted lines of whose drapery create a rich decorative effect. The woman is bringing an offering to the tomb, which consists of steps—on which are laid little wreaths and ritual vases—leading up to the stele, now unmarked as if the deceased portrayed thereon had descended for a moment, called by love to live again.

The almost palpable silence engulfing the two protagonists of this scene unquestionably emanates from the bare white background of this tall slender vase whose outline is taken up again and enhanced by the spare lines of the tomb, the great participant in this unforgettable scene.

PAINTER OF THE BOSANQUET VASE
Lekythos with Young Woman Honoring the Tomb of a Hero
Ca. 440 B.C.
Height 18⅞".
(1935)

ATTIC SCULPTOR. *Relief ot the Fallen Warrior.*   *p. 126*
This high relief was part of a monument erected by the Athenians in the Polyandron to commemorate the cavalrymen who died in the battles of Corinth and Koroneias (394 B.C.) and whose names were inscribed on the base.

Also from the Polyandron was an entablature with palm and acanthus leaves, lotus flowers, rosettes and Corinthian spiral scrolls (no. 754; width, 7'4½") raised in the center and sloping down on the sides, crowning a sepulchral monument that also bears the inscribed names of the Athenians who died in those battles. Among the latter was Dexileos to whom was dedicated the stupendous mortuary stele now in the Kerameikos Museum.

This relief with the cavalryman about to strike a fallen enemy takes its inspiration from the majestic examples of the Parthenon friezes and, generally speaking, from the great sculpture of the fifth century. The intense rhythm of the transverse, converging forms of the fallen warrior and the horse and the parallel movements of the onlooker and rider are the real protagonists that create the passionate and vehement "temperature" of the spectacle.

REED PAINTER (?). *Lekythos with Deceased Soldier before His Own Tomb,* detail.   *p. 127*
Both this lekythos and its companion no. 1816 also in the Athens Museum were discovered in Eretria and have very similar figurations. The technique employed is identical: that of a master who is usually identified as the Reed Painter who, with the Achilles Painter, was the outstanding personality creating this particular and expressive type of pottery. These lekythoi can be attributed to him or—as some critics claim—to a no less important, but immediate, follower. They serve as significant proof of the search for a "functional line" creating those deep

124

planes, distances and rhythms that were to characterize their pictorial language.

The line is the sole aesthetic entity existing on the smooth compact surface that this particular type of vase offers to the decorator: a lengthened cylinder of limited diameter with a sharp curvature at the base of the very narrow neck. The images of the soldier dejectedly sitting in front of his own tomb and of the onlookers and mourners, depend solely on the flowing line; and its flux alone suggests volumes (thorax, thighs), foreshortenings (hands), shadows, transparencies and, in animation, even coherent personal feelings. The brief touches of color seem to be casual and sometimes incongruous in the exceptionally refined play of rapid and spontaneous brushstrokes, which attain an extraordinary emotional intensity, remarkable even in this period of great figurative creativity. Tired, alone, and without further hope, the deceased abandons himself to his own sorrow and regrets for a life that the observing figures near him represent, but which is now definitely lost.

P. 127
MASTER OF THE REEDS(?)
Lekythos with Deceased Soldier Before his Own Tomb, detail
End fifth century B.C.
Height 19¼".
From Eretria. (1817)

TIMOTHEOS(?). *Aura, or Nereid(?), on Horseback.*   *p. 128, left*
This akroterion (ornamental finial) is one of the sculptures in Parian marble from the Doric Temple of Asklepios at Epidauros, which most probably was

Below
ATTIC SCULPTOR
Relief of the Fallen Warrior
394 B.C.
Height 23½".
From Athens. (2744)

built between 380 and 370 B.C., the latter year being the date of its completion. All of these sculptures, found during the excavations begun in 1881 at the site, are now preserved in the Athens Museum. We know the names of several of the artists and the subjects of the decorations thanks to the numerous surviving inscriptions; but the latter are so fragmentary and full of gaps as to deny us the possibility of identifying with certainty the work of the individual masters who are mentioned.

This figure seated on the powerful horse—presumably emerging from the sea and portraying a nymph of the air or of the sea—was part of the decoration of the temple. It belongs intrinsically to the post-Pheidian school of sculpture that was still exceptionally vigorous at the beginning of the fourth century. But, as has been noted, it shows a different sensitivity to the problems of rhythm, which is no longer as fluent and continuous as in the "classical" works of the preceding century, but is broken up and takes different directions and assumes varying movements, as can be clearly observed in the drapery.

It is generally believed that this statue was the work of the sculptor Timotheos, who certainly was the principal master and source of inspiration of this temple, thus playing the same role as Pheidias for the Parthenon, of whom Timotheos proved a persuasive and faithful interpreter.

Below Left
TIMOTHEOS(?)
Aura, or Nereid(?), on Horseback
Ca. 380–370 B.C.
Marble; height 31¼".
From Epidauros. (157)

Below right
HEKTORIDAS(?)
Amazon on Horseback
Ca. 380–370 B.C.
Height 30¾".
From Epidauros. (136)

HEKTORIDAS(?). *Amazon on Horseback.*   *p. 128, right*

This moving fragment is one of the figures from the west pediment of the Temple of Asklepios at Epidauros, in which was depicted an *Amazonomachia* (Battle of the Amazons), as distinguished from the east pediment, in which the *Plunder of Troy* was the subject. The robust figure, placed with force on the nobly modeled horse has been recognized by some scholars as the Queen of the Amazons, Pentesilea. Holes bored into the figure and in the animal itself indicate that the bridle and the reins were of metal. Even within the general unity of the pictorial language it is felt that the more dramatic compositions and the more powerful modeling that characterizes some of the fragments of the pediments must be attributed not to Timotheos himself but to the second sculptor listed in the inscription, Hektoridas, who has been recognized as an interpreter of the so-called "Peloponnesian" style.

TIMOTHEOS. *Votive Relief with the God Asklepios.*   *p. 130*

This relief, which has the same delicate transparency as the Victories that embellished the frieze of the Temple of Athena Nike (Athens, Acropolis Museum, ca. 410 B.C.), offers an exceptional example for the archeological study of Greek sculpture, with its classifications and its philological and epigraphical hypotheses, which have been numerous even for the discoveries at Epidauros in general.

We know that Timotheos carved several small votive panels for the Temple of Asklepios at Epidauros. Therefore, it has been logical to attribute to him this work, which unquestionably portrays the god Asklepios. (A statue of the same divinity, also seated on a throne, the work of Thrasymedes of Paros, was in the interior of the temple and has been lost.) Another small panel, very similar in composition and in the pose of the god (no. 174), has a mutilated face, so that we cannot be certain whether it is intended to represent Asklepios or Apollo; it appears more contracted in its identical but lengthened seated position; and the sharper and more incisive folds of the mantle are gathered together in symmetrical groups and undulations quivering with repressed vitality. We know that two other artists—in addition to the previously mentioned Hektoridas— worked on the decorations. But only four letters of the name of one of them have survived—"Theo"—and he has been identified variously as Theodotos, Theotimos or, more probably, Theon.

The Asklepios of this relief is generally believed to be one of the certain works of Timotheos, who in the inscription is named as the principal artist and inspirer of all the decorations. The luminous and masterful development of the figure within the fluent swirls of the soft folds seem to confirm this attribution. The most recent hypotheses presume that Timotheos was of Ionic or insular origin and that he brought with him to Athens, to the Peloponnesos and to Pergamon—where he most definitely was active—those refinements of form that were characteristic of the so-called "Insular" style. We can also note the very strong and incisive presence of the post-Pheidian tradition: the attentive and intelligent experimentation with thin and delicately transparent drapery; the expressive intensity of the poses and physiognomies of such nobly developed figures. Many critics, in fact, have been induced to consider him a precursor, if not actually the master of Skopas.

ATTIC ARTIST. *Commemorative Relief of the Alliance between Athens and Korkyra (Corfu).* *p. 131*

The high steles carved to commemorate outstanding events in the lives of the cities had a small frieze in relief epitomizing the occasion above larger panels on which were engraved the clauses of a treaty or the text of a law.

This stele was erected on the south side of the Acropolis—where it was found—and celebrates the treaty of alliance between Athens and Corfu personified by the two female figures in the center and on the right. The elderly seated man with whom Corfu is conversing is Eretteos, who symbolizes the people of Athens. The attributes of the goddess Athena at far right—the shield and the spear—were originally painted on the background of the relief.

The alliance was signed in 375–374 B.C. and this fact offers us a definite date for the sculpture. Since we must presume that the work was commissioned and executed immediately after the conclusion of the pact, we can date this relief with certainty in the history of Greek sculpture.

This work and, in general, the other commemorative reliefs—many of which are also in the Athens Museum—which can be dated with absolute certainty are often employed as indisputable points of reference for dating other sculptures of

TIMOTHEOS
Votive Relief with the God Asklepios
Ca. 380 B.C.
Height 25¼".
From Epidauros. (173)

130

ATTIC ARTIST
*Commemorative Relief of the Alliance Between
Athens and Korkyra (Corfu)*
374 B.C.
Height 14⅝".
From Athens. (1467)

the fourth century. It must be remembered, however, that the steles were the work of expert artisans who, having received a commission from the city, took up again and repeated compositional forms and solutions that the more famous masters had already exploited and transcended.

The craftsman responsible for this relief of 374 B.C. resorted to a mixture of styles without particular originality, but he spoke an educated language that reveals average taste yet with elevated aims.

SKOPAS. *Head of a Soldier with Attic Helmet.*   *p. 133*

Together with the following work, this *Head of a Soldier* came from a temple in Tegea dedicated to Athena Alea, a famous fifth-century sanctuary destroyed by fire in 395/394 B.C. and rebuilt under the supervision of Skopas to whom, at the present time, these two heads are attributed together with two others: no. 179 in the Athens Museum; and the *Head of the Kalydonian Boar,* no. 178 in the Museum of Tegea.

It is impossible today to reconstruct architectonically the temple of Tegea because it was totally destroyed. The surviving smashed fragments do not permit us to visualize a satisfying image of its sculptural decorations, and therefore of the work of the great sculptor from Paros who, as we know from the literature of antiquity, was a man of intense and even anguished emotion—a substantial proof of which is offered by the few surviving fragments. Skopas has in fact been held responsible for that decisive moment in the history of Greek art when "the emergence of passionate emotions eliminated classical restraint." If the work of the master—active in the years between 370 and 355 B.C.—cannot be identified with absolute certainty, it seems justifiable to recognize his hand in these

P. 133
SKOPAS
Head of a Soldier with Attic Helmet
370–355 B.C.
Marble; height 12⅝".
From Tegea. (180)

Left
SKOPAS(?)
Head of Woman (Hygeia ?)
Ca. 360 B.C.
Marble; height 11¼".
From Tegea. (3602)

miserable broken fragments of the facade sculptures which represented *The Struggle Between Achilles and Telephos* and *The Kalydonian Boar Hunt.* They are documents that prove the presence of a very strong and definitely innovating personality revealing new aspects of artistic sensitivity and demolishing, in the wake of the still timid attempts of Timotheos, the compact Olympian serenity of fifth-century sculpture in order to introduce strongly pathetic forms.

In this head of a hoplite the squared structure, the synthetic execution of the details—the volutes of which resemble the spiral scrolls of architecture—the pronounced planes with their abrupt passages from one to another, the strong plastic contrasts of light and shadow all emphasize the passionate intensity of the artist. To these elements must be added the modifications in the anatomical treatment of such features as the hollow eye-sockets, the broken facial planes, and the torsion of the head.

SKOPAS(?). *Head of a Woman (Hygeia?).* p. 132
According to many students, this head, which was also found on the site of the Temple of Athena Alea, could not have been a part of the work carried out by Skopas. In the serenity of the flowing and majestic modeling, these experts have discovered clear references to the coloristic taste of Praxiteles in the years around 360–350 B.C.

We are unable to exclude the possibility that in that period the expressive forms of Praxiteles and Skopas joined, even if they did not fuse. Yet, in truth, this feminine head—still most beautiful even in its poor state of preservation—displays in its circumscribed and austere structure and emotional intensity a definite severance from the calm serenity and grace of Praxiteles. We do not know today whether the emotional power that Skopas demonstrated in other heads of the pediments of Tegea declined into passionate sorrow; or whether the grief was restrained and sublimated with elegiac, and not solely dramatic accents. That certainly is the case in the soft visage of this woman, which may be the head of the statue of the goddess Hygeia mentioned in Pausanias as being within the Temple (the body discovered in recent excavations is now the subject of close examination and discussion).

BRYAXIS. *Horseman Approaching a Tripod.* p. 135
The large squared block discovered near the Theseion of Athens has three very similar figures of horsemen in relief on three sides; on the fourth there is an inscription commemorating the victories of the three men portrayed: Demainetos, Demeas, Demosthenes—father and two sons. It also mentions the fact that both the reliefs and the votive equestrian statue surmounting it were the work of Bryaxis. We know that the sculptor was already famous around 350 B.C., when he worked with Skopas on the decorations of the Mausoleum of Halikarnassos; but this is the only work that can be attributed to him with certainty. We are justified in presuming that we must attribute to the artist not only the lost statue that was mounted on the block but also the execution—or, at least, the supervision of the work—of the dynamic reliefs of the base, which must have reflected the more important part above.

Works like this and many others prove that the Greeks had a long tradition of interest in animals, and particularly the horse as a functional organism endowed with aesthetic characteristics or, in other words, proportions. As a result there arose not only the human "canon" but also the equestrian "canon," with its geometric formulas, which stimulated the development of humanistic culture, notable in later times in the work of Leonardo da Vinci and Albrecht Dürer.

PRAXITELEAN SCULPTOR. *Apollo and Marsyas; Three Muses.*   p. 137
These are two of three surviving side panels of a base, found in Mantineia in 1887, on which were mounted the statues of Leto, Apollo, and Artemis in the temple dedicated to Leto and her children. (The third relief also portrays three muses, but is badly damaged.) They correspond perfectly to the description Pausanias gave of them: "Praxiteles made their statues in the third generation after Alkamenes; on the base which supports them are represented the Muses and Marsyas playing the flute." The fourth relief, which is lost, probably portrayed the other three Muses.

It can be taken for granted that, if these reliefs on the base were not the work of the master himself to whom was attributed the group of the three more important figures, they were at least the products of his workshop and most probably executed on the basis of his inspiration or even drawings. In fact, although the execution is perfunctory, we find again here the explicit element of the artistic language of the years around 360 B.C.—the investigation of the infinite possibilities of rhythm offered by the movement of the human body. In the central scene of Apollo and Marsyas in particular—with a metrical relationship of 1:2—we can note the static grandeur and assurance of the seated

Apollo, which is in sharp contrast to the lively geometry and tension of the Marsyas and the impassive figure of Scita. Even the Muses offer a sort of repertory of cadenced poses in which one can discover a new solidarity in the flexible and pliant bodies, with the drapery sublimating in tranquil serenity the original agitation of Pheidias.

ATTIC SCULPTOR (EUPHRANOR?). *Youth from Antikythera.* p. 138–139
This bronze was found in 1900 in the sea off the small island of Antikythera south of the Peloponnesos peninsula, together with other precious works of a later period. They were undoubtedly all part of a cargo of art treasures being transported to Rome in the first century and lost in a shipwreck.

The youth with fiery eyes made of inserted semiprecious stones has been variously identified as Perseus lifting the head of the Medusa, Herakles in the garden of the Hesperides, or Paris awarding the golden apple to Venus. The statue has been attributed by some to Lysippos, on the basis of the attention given to the vibrant athletic anatomy and the innovating, unstable balance of the figure represented in a moment of precarious, instantaneous, diagonal equilibrium: the left arm and leg firm and tense; the right arm and leg raised in motion, angled in a similar manner but in opposite directions, both vertically and horizontally, and forward and backward.

The connection with Praxitelean form is, however, equally explicit: the consideration given to the external relationships with the environment as, for example, in the spatial positioning of the arms with the evident intention of creating a third dimension; and in the handling of light which, through the plastic softness of the modeling, slips over the body creating expressive effects of chiaroscuro.

The proposed identification of the figure as Paris—accepted by many—has induced critics to assume that it is a documented work of the sculptor Euphranor in which he is said to have represented in a single figure "the judge of the goddesses, the lover of Helen and the slayer of Achilles." Even if we accept the judgment of the historians—who generally prove to be quite penetrating when they find comfort in a specific work to which they can refer—it would still seem erroneous to find in this masterpiece of beauty and innovating, constructive tension the hand of a "versatile" sculptor, a "conscientious" theorist of the problems of symmetry, a creator of figures "of flesh and blood." These definitions can correspond to the work only if they are interpreted as assertions of positive praise expressed in commonplace terms. The most widely accepted date of execution transfers the original hypothesis of the beginning of the century to ca. 340 B.C.

ATTIC SCULPTOR. *Boy from Marathon.*   pp. 140–141
This magnificent bronze, recently recovered from the sea in the Bay of Marathon, was probably lost in a shipwreck. It is an outstanding original work, manifesting the diffusion and widespread influence of Praxitelean art in Attica, as can be seen in the controlled rhythm and the dynamic equilibrium of the unidentified personage. Devoid of any recognizable attribute—with eyes of white hardstone and dark glass—the youth fixes his attention on a flat object held in his extended hand. He has therefore been variously identified as Apollo Sauroktonos, Hermes, or Satyr Pouring Wine.

Attributed by some scholars directly to Praxiteles himself or, at least, to his school as a late work of ca. 330 B.C., it certainly followed in the wake of the great Attic master. Yet, the solid features, the rounded body and the precise action of the muscles are clear indications of the Lysippian experience. It must accordingly be the work of a solitary elaborator of inherited traditions, fusing and

strengthening them in the last decades of the century.

Finally, note must be made that, in view of the undoubted influence of the Praxitelean school, some historians maintain that the statue was the work of one of the master's two sons—Kephisodotos or Timarchos—who are known to have followed in the footsteps of their father.

ATTIC ARTIST (SILANION?). *Head of a Boxer.*   *p. 143*
The remains of a crown of olive leaves indicate that this head, found in Olympia, was that of a victorious boxer. In view of the extraordinary physiognomic vivacity of this magnificent bronze, the hypothesis has been put forward that it may have been the work of the sculptor Silanion in the 113 Olympiad (ca. 328 B.C.). He is thought to have been active between approximately 350 and 320 B.C. Among the numerous creations of the artist, his Roman and Greek contempo-

Left, detail right
ATTIC SCULPTOR (EUPHRANOR ?)
Youth from Antikythera
Ca. 340 B.C.
Bronze; height 76⅜".
(13396)

138

Left, detail right
ATTIC SCULPTOR
Boy from Marathon
Ca. 330 B.C.
Bronze; height 48″.
(15118)

raries mention a portrait of the athlete Satyros of Elis who, it is suggested, may be the personage presented here.

With its strong, prominent and rugged features, together with the tousled hair and bushy beard, this head is representative of an artistic ideal in which nature is equated with physical, personal existence—the exaltation of vital force and its manifestation in uncontrollable eruption.

ATTIC SCULPTOR. *Stele of Father and Son.*   *p. 142, left*

Perhaps the most poignant of the stupendous scenes of farewell among the Greek funerary steles that have been bequeathed to us is this superb example found in the bed of the river Ilissos near Athens.

The two figures close together, in a relief so deep that they are almost in the full round, are isolated one from the other. Yet they are clearly linked both in elevation—the vertical of the elder, the diagonal of the youth—and in the

P. 143
ATTIC SCULPTOR (SILANION?)
Head of a Boxer, detail
Ca. 330 B.C.
Bronze; height 10¼".
From Olympia. (6439)

Lower left
ATTIC SCULPTOR
Stele of Father and Son
Ca. 340 B.C.
Height 5' 6½".
From Ilissos. (869)

Lower right
ATTIC SCULPTOR
Grave Stele of Aminokleia
First half fourth century B.C.
Height 4' 5½".
From Piraeus. (718)

plane—the steps, feet and dog converge in front of the parallels traced by the perpendicular elements. In such an architectonically conceived composition, the little weeping slave and the dog fail to disturb the grave and contemplative atmosphere. The splendid, luminous presence of the deceased youth is tranquil and unimpaired; and the old father facing him on the right seems to be engrossed in meditation. Death is not tragic, but a human or fateful vicissitude to be accepted with stoic rationality that knows the limits of existence. Already famous at the time of its execution, of which the number of surviving replicas gives ample proof, this stele has been generally dated about 340 B.C., and has often been attributed to the great Skopas on the basis of the intensity of feeling. It is one of the first steles in which the figures were carved almost in the full round, moving on a shallow proscenium. As in the *Stele of Aristonautes* and *The Sisters,* the composition is organized with the equivalent of pictorial perspective.

ATTIC SCULPTOR. *Grave Stele of Aminokleia.*   *p. 142, right*
Found at Piraeus in 1836, this funerary monument has been attributed to the Master of the Ctesileos and Theanos Stele (no. 3472, the Athens Museum). But another hypothesis formulated by some critics seems more probable, namely that it is a copy of a lost original of which there exists in the Museum a fragment of yet another, later, copy (no. 2042). As in the case of the Stele of Hegeso (p. 119) and its copies with variations, there is also the possibility that there was a workshop of a very high aesthetic and technical level that produced replicas of models supplied by great masters.

The rigid and impersonal execution, indeed, appears to be unrelated in its lack of precision, to the highly emotional quality of the poignant scene infused with the sorrow of a moment of final farewell. The deceased, already veiled for the departure, and the two handmaids, whose almost fully rounded heads are in contrast with their bodies which are merely indicated by the undulations of their draperies, are placed at right and left of the panel with a compositional rhythm that is incongruous in the small space in which they are placed. The youthful round arm of Aminokleia, pathetically caressing the head of the kneeling maiden tying her sandal, is the sole element linking the two groups, and the only noncurvilinear motif—with a definite diagonal direction—in this exceptional compositional masterpiece. It is generally believed that the Master of the Aminokleia Stele worked in the first half of the fourth century.

ATTIC SCULPTOR. *Grave Stele of Philinos.*   *p. 145*
During the fourth century the funerary steles, already numerous, were amplified and enriched with a multiplication of figures, while the environment within which they were contained was rendered with greater complexity. They were produced in many specialized workshops and reflected the language of several masters who supervised their production and often supplied models of high artistic quality up to the time of Demetrios of Phaleron who, in 317 B.C., issued an "anti-luxury" decree that imposed sobriety in sculptured gravestones and such a sharp limitation on available materials that this particular form of artistic expression rapidly declined and soon disappeared.

This gravestone, found in Athens, is of a less frequent type with its representation of four figures. Another, compositionally very similar, also in the same Museum (no. 743), has a perfectly preserved encasement which gives a better idea of the articulated arrangement of the group and its relationship with the external world beyond the limits of the narrow space within which it is set.

It seems that the name of the deceased was Philinos; according to reliable sources this name was inscribed on a pediment surmounting the stele that a long

ATTIC SCULPTOR
Grave Stele of Philinos(?)
340 B.C.
Height 70⅞".
From Athens. (832)

time ago was in a private collection, but has since been lost. The absence of the architectonic elements permits us now to analyze clearly the triangular structure of the composition of the four figures placed obliquely on the proscenium in that version of perspective that was later to be called "on the angle." Two of the figures are carved almost in full round: the deceased already detached from human passions and seated in profile, and the noblewoman a little further back on the right—still a Pheidian type—turned in an oblique movement toward the background. The arms of the two are joined in a farewell handshake, and intensely sorrowful glances are exchanged between them. The bust of the husband behind in half-relief serves as the central axis of the composition. Also in half-relief, the lovely head of the servant at left is supported by her right arm in the attitude of a dispassionate spectator.

This gravestone has been linked stylistically to the slightly earlier masterpiece of the *Father and Son* from Ilissos (p. 142), which has been attributed to Skopas. Once again in this work we find the same noble forms and emotional intensity in a sculpturally more complicated, even overloaded figuration, stressing the concept of the stoic acceptance of inevitable destiny, painfully suffered.

ATTIC SCULPTOR. *Stele of Farewells (Leave-taking of Two Sisters).*   *p. 147, left*

This stele is another example (from Athens) almost in full-round high-relief. The projection from the background is emphasized by the oblique forward position of the chair on which the deceased sits, leaning toward the young woman from whom she must be permanently separated. The arms of the two figures are united in a horizontal movement of solid volumetric composition; and an even stronger element of unity is the spiritual climate that emanates from the intense glances of the faces and the singularly melancholic features of the two heads with their accents of pathos. The bodies are wrapped in drapery with deeply engraved folds that merely suggest the underlying volumes. The timid maid in the far left corner is present only in limited dimensions and with minor evidence in the relief, as if she were dazed by the premature farewell. Clearly the work of a great sculptor, active about 340 B.C., this stele now lacks its original architectonic frame, which must have been in the form of a very deep niche surmounted by a pediment, in order to contain the scene in an intimate, recollected setting, wherein the contrasts of light and shade would be attenuated in a fused and filtered atmosphere.

ATTIC SCULPTOR. *Grave Stele of Plangon.*   *p. 147, right*

Found at Oropos in Boeotia, the gravestone that Tolmides of Plateas dedicated to his wife Plangon reveals an aspect that was rare in this type of artistic creation: carved in very high relief, it depicts a realistic death scene.

The position of the young deceased, the dramatic agitation of the attending women, and the attitude of the husband, seem to indicate that Plangon died in childbirth.

Generally dated about 340 B.C. the stele was realized in a sculptural language frequently found in votive reliefs and particularly in commemorative panels of modest dimensions, consisting simply of a slab surmounted by a pediment. Rather than carved, the scene was engraved without too much attention being given to questions of beauty, but with a compositional rigor that can be observed, for example, in the ascending movement of the ground planes: from left to right, Tolmides standing on the floor, the first maid standing on a raised

146

Below left
ATTIC SCULPTOR
Stele of Farewells
(Leave-taking of Two Sisters)
Ca. 340 B.C.
Height 67".
From Athens. (870)

Below right
ATTIC SCULPTOR
Funerary Stele of Plangon
Ca. 340 B.C.
Height 30¾".
From Oropos. (832)

platform, the dying woman extended on the bed on a still higher level, and the scene terminated at right by the fourth figure standing on the floor, in profile and vertically like the husband at left with whom she shares the function of concluding the narration. Exceptional as a dramatic, authentic document of a grief-stricken event, the relief, maintaining modalities of an earlier graphic-pictorial style, stands out as an anomalous example among other fourth-century steles with its own agitated language and its extraordinary depiction of a tragic daily occurrence that is far different from the stoicism and the sorrowful acceptance that characterize the customary steles of farewell.

ATTIC SCULPTURE. *Stele of Husband and Wife.*   *p. 148, left*
Even in the final years of the steles, with their prodigious flowering and contemporaneously with the more complex family scenes, there still appeared some depicting in a few simple forms the final farewell. Thus in this Attic stele, discovered at Rhamnous and dated about 320 B.C., the figures of husband and wife are separated in such a way as to become almost two single isolated statues carved in the round, yet bound together by the intensity of their reciprocal glances. The composition is deliberately divided into two distinct parts, different in form and pose as well as in the rhythm and dynamics: the body of the man is broken up, angular, with the left leg crossing the right; the female figure columnar and frontal, traversed by the fluent diagonals of the mantle.

It appears evident that the artist was inspired by the analogous conception of

Lower left
ATTIC SCULPTOR
Stele of Husband and Wife
Ca. 320 B.C.
Height 69".
From Rhamnous. (833)

Lower right
ATTIC SCULPTOR
Grave Stele of Prokleides
Ca. 330 B.C.
Height 31½".
From Athens. (737)

148

the *Father and Son* stele found in the Ilissos River (p. 142), which had been executed a few decades earlier. The bodies of the couple with their slender proportions and their nobly ideal heads are a prelude to the beauty of the sculpture of the third century B.C.

ATTIC SCULPTOR. *Grave Stele of Prokleides.*   *below, right*

Brought to light in the Kerameikos of Athens, this funerary monument still bears traces of polychrome decoration: a red background and blue drapery. The restored frame permits us to appreciate fully the values of the chiaroscuro conceived by the sculptor when he created the work about 330 B.C.

The farewell between the soldier and the bearded deceased takes place in deeper space than usual: the two figures are carved in the round, whereas the woman—mother or wife—emerges only slightly from the background despite the deeply carved folds of her mantle.

As has been observed in preceding steles, the figures in height and on the planes are composed in an opposition between a structural block with a cubic base (the father) and a diagonal volume (the soldier) which intersects the scene and unites the two with the oblique link of the handshake. It is a composition that is rigorously unified by internal connections in a variety of views, interpenetrations and shifts of direction, giving a spontaneous, dramatic effect. A sculptural *mise en scène* of this type had many novel variations in the contemporary sculpture of steles.

ATTIC SCULPTOR. *Grave Stele of Aristonautes.*   *p. 150*

The sole protagonist of this large almost intact gravestone is Aristonautes, who emerges from the shadowy recess of the niche with dynamic impetus. The violent forward movement of the body is further emphasized by the agitated slanting folds of the clothing. This single figure of a soldier posed for assault against an invisible enemy is almost a depiction of valor beyond place and time.

Carved practically in the full round—almost an isolated statue—and quite evidently inspired by Lysippos' warrior groups, the figure is united to the background on the left by the incised swirling folds of the chlamys, while on the right the flowing drapery extends the impetuous movement of the soldier by harmonizing the folds with the brisk pace forward.

Generally and justifiably believed to be one of the last of the "sumptuous" gravestones executed prior to the issuance of the "anti-luxury" decree, this was certainly the work of one of the great sculptors of the end of the fourth century. The passion concentrated in the body and the deep eyes in shadow, together with the dynamic intensity of the composition, have persuaded some scholars to date the sculpture in the first half of the century and to attribute it to Timotheos or, at least, to a predecessor of Skopas.

In this work the three-dimensional setting is perfectly realized: it is constructed with a deep recess and, in certain lighting the background is thrown into partial or total obscurity, creating limitless space; on the other hand, the light striking the figure gives it a powerful life-giving energy, emphasizing its emerging lateral movement.

HELLENISTIC GOLDSMITH. *Medallion with Female Bust (Artemis?).*

p. 151, top

A "treasure" of the goldwork found at Karditsa in Thessaly, which passed from private hands to the Athens Museum, exemplifies the refinement and sobriety of Hellenistic toreutics. The individual objects—among which is a *naiskos* (medallion) showing *Dionysos and a Satyr*—have been variously dated: according to some experts, the middle of the third century; according to others, the second century B.C., on the assumption that a repetition of models can justifiably be traced back to the third century.

Set like a gem within the series of concentric ornamental bands, this bust portrays a divinity—probably Artemis—emerging with its head in the round,

P. 151, top
HELLENISTIC GOLDSMITH
Medallion with Female Bust (Artemis ?)
Ca. 250 B.C.
Gold; diam. 9¹⁄₁₆".
From Karditsa. (369)

P. 151, below
CHAIRESTRATOS
Themis
Beginning of third century B.C.
Marble; height 86⅝".
From Rhamnous. (231)

ATTIC SCULPTOR
Grave Stele of Aristonautes
Ca. 320 B.C.
Marble; height 84".
(738)

150

proudly erect on a cylindrical, slightly turning neck. The folds of the dress enliven the circular setting of the medallion, held in a delicate network of chains with a freedom of movement which heightens the elegance of this rare piece, reflecting the fastidious taste of a refined culture.

The frequent use of human or animal motifs, the predilection for filigree, and the transposition into gold of the same opulent form language animating the great contemporary sculpture are some of the characteristics of the art of the Hellenistic goldsmiths. We do not know what use was made of this *naiskos* or any of the other large medallions in the "Treasure of Thessaly," of which this is probably the most original piece. It has been suggested that they might have been employed as covers for circular boxes.

CHAIRESTRATOS. *Themis*   *left*

This austere figure of a young woman wrapped in a heavy peplos is an image of the goddess Themis, dedicated to her by Megakles, son of Megakles, in the Temple of Nemesis in Rhamnous, and signed by the sculptor Chairestratos. The latter was active around 315 B.C. and was representative of a generation of provincial artists who toward the end of the century still admired the great examples of rigor and nobility left by the masters of the fifth and fourth centuries. They interpreted these with such dignity as to arrive at a point of almost academic eclecticism in explicit references to Pheidias, Praxiteles and Lysippos.

Too few elements remain at our disposal—a fragment of a head, presumed images on coins—to permit us to decide whether the Nemesis that Agorakritos, favorite disciple of Pheidias, executed for the same temple in Rhamnous influenced Chairestratos when working on this great statue around 290 B.C. What is certain is that the pose and the thick folds of the chiton and the himation are almost identical with those of the statue in the British Museum which Artemisia erected alongside that of her husband in the Mausoleum of Halikarnassos. This celebrated monument had been a meeting point of the most important sculptors in the middle of the fourth century: Skopas, Timotheos, Bryaxis, Leochares.

As with other contemporary female figures, the body of this statue is employed as a mobile agent which—through its varying postures of immobility, equilibrium, movement—distributes and composes the draperies as they drop, envelop and flow flexibly with great elegance and even, at times, with a superfluity of chiaroscuro.

ATTIC SCULPTOR. *Ethiopian with Horse.*   *p. 152*

Found in Athens, this magnificent relief consisting of two marble slabs joined together was most probably part of a funerary monument in honor of some illustrious personage. The traces of color—black on the face of the groom and the back of the horse, red in the hair of the boy—indicate that this superb fragment from a group which must have been colossal is in some way linked with the fourth-century funerary steles.

The work has been attributed to a great master of the beginning of the third century, on the basis of the explicit references to more ancient prototypes, especially the geometric composition with complete integration of individual parts; the latter, however, are individually emphasized almost to the point of

ATTIC SCULPTOR
Ethiopian with Horse
Beginning of third century B.C.
Marble; height 78¾".
From Athens. (4464)

conflict. It is a representation of energies in a state of explosive tension disciplined by a rigorous dominating power.

HELLENISTIC SCULPTOR. *Portrait of an Old Man (Philosopher?). p. 153*
This is a notable example of portraiture in the Hellenistic period which was often strongly marked by virtuoso realism combined with a predilection for luminous pictorial values. The head has been dated from both the third and the second centuries B.C., but the earlier dating seems to be the more plausible. It was found near the small island of Antikythera (Lakonia), in a cargo of art treasures shipped to Rome and lost at sea, from which it was fortuitously recovered some two thousand years later.

The bronze in this case has suffered but not to such an extent as to alter the formal values peculiar to the work. The sharp characterization of the ironic and mordant physiognomy of this head is so pronounced that one is led to see in the tense, repressed, almost sly visage the image of a Cynic-philosopher. Some scholars have even identified it as the portrait of an actual person, Bion of Borysthenes, third-century B.C., philosopher known for his caustic sayings.

Among the many fragments found on the site of the shipwreck were two

152

bronze feet, an arm and a piece of a himation which some students believe belonged to the same statue; but the doubts regarding the dating of the head are sufficient to justify archeologists' hesitations about the possibility of reconstructing the entire figure with any plausible certainty.

HELLENISTIC SCULPTOR. *Boy Jockey on Horseback.* *p. 154*
This boy with negroid features—of a type that is frequently found in Middle-Eastern art, and resembling other Greek works, such as the *Negro Boy* of the Bibliothèque Nationale, Paris—is one of the most impressive masterpieces of Hellenistic sculpture. It was found in the sea near Cape Artemision.

The reckless agility of this youngster who, having jumped on the back of the horse, makes an effort to control the reins while turning his head as if listening to cries of instruction, provided a splendid pretext for a doubly centrifugal composition. The arms and legs explode in alternate rhythms and opposite directions from the axis of the body. Modeled with terse vigor and essential energy, the limbs and torso seem to fly apart. And the keen yet guileless face of

HELLENISTIC SCULPTOR
Portrait of an Old Man (Philosopher ?)
Third or second (?) century B.C.
Bronze; height 11⅜".
From Antikythera. (13400)

153

the boy protrudes from the fragile diminutive body with urgent, burning emotional tension.

The dating is uncertain, the most plausible hypotheses oscillating between 240 and 150 B.C. It is a work which manifests the vast exchanges of diverse artistic languages that were opened to Greek figurative culture—from Syria to the Aegean Islands, from Pergamon to Alexandria—in what is generally called the Hellenistic period, extending from the death of Alexander in 323 B.C. to the Roman conquest of Egypt in 31 B.C. The period was too long and the area too vast to make it possible to fix the moment and place in which an exceptionally gifted artist might have created this masterpiece.

The superb horse is life-size and likewise creates an unforgettable impression. It was reconstructed from fragments found in the depths of the sea in the same area as the figure of the boy. It may not have been originally a part of the group—most critics consider it to be a work of the fourth century—but it could have been adopted by the sculptor of the jockey at a later epoch to complete this extraordinary tour de force. But the dimensional, compositional and formal unity of the horse and boy is so explicit that we lean to the hypothesis of a single, simultaneous creation. The incredible impetus that lengthens and projects the large nervous body of the race horse, the suffering and panting nostrils pointed toward the goal, and the protruding muscles contracted in vehement vibrations of light and shade are the real protagonists of this extraordinary image suspended in midair in a moment of final leap to victory.

HELLENISTIC SCULPTOR
Boy Jockey on Horseback
Third or second (?) century B.C.
Bronze; height of boy 32″; height
of horse 90½″.
From Cape Artemision. (15177)

EUKLEIDES. *Head of Zeus.*   *p. 156, left*
This head is the only surviving fragment—together with a hand (Athens Museum no. 3487)—of a colossal statue of a seated Zeus carved by the Athenian Eukleides for the temple dedicated to the god at Aigeira in Achaia. The complete figuration is known from Roman coins struck for that city.

The strong influence of Pheidias, especially noticeable in its overall classical dignity, had persuaded some scholars to date it in the fourth or third centuries. However, this is too early a period because Eukleides—mentioned by Pausanias who saw the statue at a much later date—was an artist with academic tastes who worked within traditional conventions like others of the second century B.C. These artists adopted the forms and tastes of the Hellenistic era at its height, and belonged to the so-called Neo-Attic school, of which Chairestratos was one of the chief exponents (p. 151).

The tradition of the colossal bearded heads of Zeus, of the type of the one of Otricoli in Italy, for example, was respected with formal accuracy in this work which, however, repressed the latent dynamics inherent in the visage. The head clearly reveals an undue attention to "realistic" factors united to an ostentatious opulence notable in the bulky, superabundant beard derived from the art of Pergamon. It is a sculpture of enormous dimensions, destined to do homage to a divinity who was assumed to exercise transcendent power, and with its open glaring eyes, which are now lost, must have had a spectacular effect.

HELLENISTIC ARTIST. *Poseidon.* *lower right*

Brought to light on the island of Melos, this imposing figure was the work of an artist of the first half of the second century and, therefore, a contemporary of the author of the renowned *Venus of Milo* now in the Louvre. This gigantic work has also enjoyed enormous fame and it undoubtedly was one of the preferred prototypes of Roman statuary.

Here we have further proof of the exchanges of influence and the relationships between the sculptors of the Aegean islands and of the flourishing culture of Pergamon in the third and the beginning of the second centuries B.C. Elements clearly derived from Skopas and Lysippos were appropriated with a vehement dramatic taste for strong plastic development which at times declined into intellectually refined forms, as exemplified in the grandiose frieze of the famous Pergamon Altar, which is the ultimate expression of that tendency.

In this statue, the powerful body emerges from thick clumps of drapery arranged in such a way as to form a sort of tidal reflux. This majestic but somewhat theatrical art rests on a careful balancing of alternating equilibriums of the torso and the limbs. The geometrical arrangement of the latter has a typical, somewhat didactic, character in its development from the falling axis of the now missing trident to the articulated axis of the figure.

The dolphin—symbol of the most important divinity of the sea—rises vertically and parallel to the right leg in such a way as to constitute a stable

Lower left
EUKLEIDES
Head of Zeus
Marble; height 34¼".
From Aigeira. (3377)

Lower right
HELLENISTIC SCULPTOR
Poseidon
First half second century B.C.
Marble; height 85⅜".
From Melos. (235)

element of support for the variegated, complex movement of the monumental body.

DAMOPHON. *Head of Anytos.*   *below*

The fragments of three heads and of a mantle (see p. 158) are all that the Athens Museum possesses of the group of colossal statues that Damophon executed for the sanctuary of Demeter and Despoina at Lykosoura. (The surviving bodies, also reduced to bits and pieces, are preserved in the local museum.) The identification is certain thanks to the precise description left us by Pausanias, who expounded at length not only on this group but also on many other works that the sculptor from Messenia—active in the first half of the second century—executed in the most important centers of the Peloponnesos. The two enthroned goddesses were flanked by two standing figures: near Demeter (fragment no. 1734) was Artemis (fragment no. 7435) in the short tunic of a huntress; alongside Despoina was the giant Anytos in the armor of a warrior. The figures were hollow, in order to lighten the excessive weight of their colossal dimensions.

These fortunately preserved fragments composing the group of Lykosoura provide evidence of an historically important moment in the development of Greek sculpture, even if it was not one of great artistic originality. In the second

DAMOPHON
Head of Anytos
First half second century B.C.
Marble; height 29⅛".
From Lykosoura. (1736)

century, especially in Hellenic territory, one can see how the revival of the taste for classical form—already important for artists like Chairestratos (p. 151)—became more intense and even excessive. This reached the point of producing good imitations which are no more than cerebral exercises, though of the highest technical level, inspired by the great models of the past.

The head of Anytos is clearly derived from the bearded portraits of the fourth century, although the artist translated his model into contemporary sculptural language, amplifying the planes on the firm underlying structure and indulging in a search for sumptuous chiaroscuro effects. The stylization of these works, bound to a criterion of intentional aesthetic imitation, established a concept and a praxis of the "classical" which, overlooking every other Greek precedent or experience, and transmitted in Roman art and, later, in the Italian Renaissance, were to become among the most important components of European artistic culture for centuries up to our time.

DAMOPHON
Mantle of Despoina, fragment
First half second century B.C.
Marble; height 44½".
From Lykosoura. (1737)

DAMOPHON. *Mantle of Despoina,* fragment.   *right*
The falling drapery held by the left arm of the goddess is a fragment of particular interest and significance. This sacred garment, here exceptionally resplendent, is embroidered with large figures in relief and bordered by wide bands with recurring ornamental motifs of flowers, cupids and animals, that fully exemplify Hellenistic taste.

The masterly technical skill with which Damophon inserted and suggested on the mobile surfaces of the mantle the rich and beautiful figurations with ingenious foreshortenings, condensations and dilations is an exercise in exaggerated virtuosity, a sort of challenge to simulate in marble the consistency, movement, cadences and undulations of a precious fabric. The taste for similar transpositions from one medium to another was not rare; it was a phenomenon that existed also in literature (onomatopoeia) and it was reminiscent of the studied contrast between an "epic" dimension and a lyrical or legendary content.

HELLENISTIC SCULPTOR (AGASIAS?). *Head of a Man.*   *p. 159, above*
This bronze head was discovered in the Arena of Delos and can be dated around 100 B.C. or, in other words, shortly before the destruction of the city by Mithridates. It has been attributed to Agasias, who was active in the early years of the first century, on the basis of a comparison with the head of the so-called *Borghese Gladiator* (Louvre) generally accepted as a work by this eclectic sculptor.

This, too, is a restatement of a great "classical" sculpture and is a typical product of Hellenistic art as it developed on the Aegean Islands where the artists created a notable quantity of original and technically qualified works. The latter were characterized by a refined virtuosity that assumed and elaborated the formalistic language of the school of Pergamon—which came to an end in the second century—by emphasizing its pathetic and at times melodramatic aspects.

The fleshy modeling of this bronze head has a capricious "pictorial" treatment in the hair, the eyebrows, and the abruptly shifting broken planes effected by brief wavy parallel incisions arranged in seemingly disordered movement. The psychological tensions derive directly from Skopas models, with their characteristic jerking forward movement, here emphasized by the protruding chin and the wrinkled forehead. This and other similar sculptures—likewise with inserted glass eyes—dating from the first century, reveal parallels with the

contemporary or slightly later Roman painting (such as in Pompeii), which did not consist simply of copies of earlier work but was a form of active participation in the cultural tradition of Hellenism, in an attempt to consolidate and perpetuate a "classical" repertory based on models that were considered to be perfect and unsurpassable.

COPYIST OF THE FIRST CENTURY FROM AN ORIGINAL OF THE FOURTH CENTURY B.C. *Dionysos and a Young Satyr.* *left, below*

This is a copy made in the imperial era from an original of the fourth century B.C. It remained unfinished and accordingly reveals the course of execution and the technique employed in the first century B.C., and in later times by both creative sculptors and copyists of original works. This consisted of establishing points of reference for the different depths of the planes. One can still see signs of the drill holes in the thick hair of the god, above the knees of both figures, and on the chest of the satyr. The surfaces having been blocked out at the predetermined depth, the form was developed with the chisel, and finally the work polished. The statue thus was brought to completion sector by sector, without submitting to the discipline of an integrated concept of the figure as a whole.

This example is of particular interest inasmuch as it is at a very advanced stage of execution. The upper part, including the back of the main figure, is almost completely liberated from the block, and the central part was ready for further operations. The artisan or artist had first of all established the essential plastic composition, whether he had a model of equal or smaller dimensions. The composition probably adhered to the original and its qualities; and the values of the original or of the model are coherent and comprehended with intelligence as compared with other solutions. There is no way of estimating how the sculptor would have resolved the final finish of the work which, aside from structural alterations, in the hands of the copyists was generally impersonal and academic.

COPYIST OF THE SECOND CENTURY, FROM AN ORIGINAL BY PHEIDIAS. *Athena Parthenos.* *p. 160, top*

The ivory and gold Athena Parthenos, which Pheidias conceived in 438 B.C. as a colossal cult image (almost fifty feet high) dedicated to the protectress of Athens, is known only in marble copies of reduced dimensions derived from the wooden model that was the only trace of the original work left after the pillage of the entire work by Lachares in 296 B.C.

The replica in the National Museum found at the Varvakeion was the heavy and generically banal work of a copyist of the second century and is today of purely iconographical interest. We do not wish to ignore it completely, however, because despite the small scale, it is the most faithful record that we have of this masterpiece by the artist who did so much to enrich his city with magnificent works and who had so much influence on the sculpture of his own epoch and that of the following centuries.

This statuette portrays the goddess wrapped in her peplos; the crest of her helmet is surmounted by a sphinx flanked by two griffins, while the enormous shield with the serpent (referring to Erittonios) rests on the ground at her left and her right hand supports the Nike, emblem of victory.

Today we can only attempt in our imagination to reconstruct the impressive richness of the original, in which more than a ton of gold was employed. All that survives are more or less authentic fragments, some of which are in this Museum: the reliefs of the base, of the interior and exterior of the shield, and even of the sandals (which were ignored in this copy). Copies like this, which perhaps reflect even indirectly the overwhelming appearance that must have characterized the colossal original, give some indication of the grandiose conception and the solemnity that Pheidias impressed on what, during his lifetime, must have been his most famous work.

COPYIST OF THE SECOND CENTURY(?) FROM THE ORIGINAL BY POLYKLEITOS. *Diadoumenos.*   *right, below*

This is a superlative copy from among the many (more than thirty) that have survived of a statue that has been identified as an image of Apollo, although others have regarded this youth binding a fillet on his head—symbol of victory—as Pythocles, an athlete who really existed.

Judging from the superior quality of the execution, this appears to be one of the earliest copies, very close to the celebrated original by Polykleitos. On the basis of its canonic perfection, this statue can be considered a completely mature work and probably the last of Polykleitos' masterpieces, as opposed to another sculpture of the master's youth, the *Doryphoros* (known from the copy in the Naples Museum). Pliny's famous antithesis between the two remains even today singularly convincing: *"molliter juvenis"* (gentle youth) vs. *"viriliter puer"* (virile looking boy). The *Diadoumenos* creates an impression of calm serenity, by the sinuous movement in the axis of the body with its ample symmetry and balanced rhythmic equilibrium, together with the soft locks of the hair billowing out from the slender fillet, and the luminously tranquil visage.

The explicitly recognized derivation from the Pheidian masterpiece of the same subject occasions a need to clarify the nature of Polykleitos' formal composition: the body is organized according to a *quadratio* (i.e., a square)—that is to say, a four-sided arrangement of the limbs, specifically a strophic turning of two opposing and two corresponding squares together forming rhythm and counterpoint—developed according to a clearly cadenced flexion of the body created by the weight on one leg, leaving the other free. We should note, however, other components of the rhythm which, as found in various other statues by Polykleitos, are imbued with the same principles, above all the semicircular crowning at the top of the statue, which in its inclination harmonizes with the circular arch of the torso. The integration of the linear elements with the plastic and conceptual elements results in a truly outstanding model.

One can justifiably assert that the rational study and canonical formulation of the problem of the athletic nude figure, which was the constant preoccupation of Polykleitos' activity, culminated in this work, datable around 430 B.C.

COPYIST OF THE SECOND CENTURY
FROM THE ORIGINAL BY PHEIDIAS
Athena Parthenos
Marble; height 3' 3⅝".
From the Varvakeion. (129)

COPYIST OF THE SECOND CENTURY (?)
FROM ORIGINAL BY POLYKLEITOS
Diadoumenos
Marble; height 6' 4¾".
(1826)

HISTORY OF THE MUSEUM
AND THE COLLECTIONS

The story of the National Archaeological Museum began with and parallels the history of modern Greece, both inspired by the rise of a national consciousness at the beginning of the nineteenth century. Even as groups in Greece and abroad began organizing to fight for independence from Turkey, a number of Athenians founded the "Society for the Lovers of the Arts." Understanding the value of ancient remains scattered throughout Greece and watching helplessly as foreign ambassadors negotiated with the occupying Turks for their removal to Northern Europe, when not simply taking or destroying antique art in some act of plunder, the Society set about recovering and storing what it could. The rallying spirit of the Society was the cultural counterpart of the patriotic spirit of the movement for the freedom of Greece. What it managed to acquire and hold in Greece would one day be part of the National Museum collections.

Once the War for Independence had secured parts of Greece, a temporary capital was established on the island of Aegina in 1828, within sight of Athens still occupied by Turkey. One of the first acts of the fledgling government was the founding of a National Museum, so named in the bill which created it in 1829. A principal object of the bill was to prohibit the export of antiquities while providing a means for the caring, storing, and display of those objects which came into the hands of the state. Immediately part of the Home for War Orphans on Aegina was turned over to the embryo collection of ancient Greek art, and in this way the physical beginning of the National Museum coincided with that of the modern Greek nation.

When Athens was liberated and made the capital in 1833, the museum was moved to the then small town, though many objects remained behind in Aegina. Its first home was the Temple of Hephaistos, then identified as the Theseion, overlooking the ancient Agora. The temple had been used as a church, but the religious furnishings were removed in 1835 to make room for the museum's art. Known as the Central Archaeological Museum, the small temple was filled within a year and more space for display and storage was required, so many of the museum pieces were moved to the Stoa of Hadrian.

By now Greece was a decade old nation with a king, Otto I, second son of the Bavarian king, and participating in European affairs while suffering its own growing pains. In Europe the nineteenth century was a century for the founding and building of great national museums, notable among many being the British Museum and National Gallery in London, the Kunsthistorisches Museum in Vienna, the National Museum in Budapest and, in Otto's home city, the Antique Museums of Munich's Königsplatz. Those museums, according to the taste of the period and logic of being homes for art, were designed in a Neoclassic style. The spirits of Iktinos and Kallikrates, the architects of the ancient Parthenon, must have smiled as architects in the entourage of King Otto arrived to design the public buildings of modern Athens in a Neoclassic style. One of the German architects was Leo von Klenze, court architect for Otto's father, the Bavarian King Ludwig. Von Klenze was the inspiration behind the Neoclassic Königsplatz in Munich and the designer of that square's temple-fronted Glyptothek Museum. In 1835 von Klenze planned a museum building for Athens in the same Neoclassic manner, but no building was begun.

Yet that a museum building was necessary grew increasingly apparent as the decades passed, for excavations and chance discoveries, along with contributions, made the collections housed in the Theseion and Stoa of Hadrian grow. And other collections around the capital sought proper care and display. Finally, in 1866 land was given for the site of a new museum which was almost immediately begun, designed by the German architect Ludwig Lange. Yet the influence of von Klenze was there, as, still today, the entrance facade of the National Museum shows a relationship to the Glyptothek in Munich.

When in 1881 the west wing of the museum building had been completed, the collections until then housed in the Theseion, the Stoa of Hadrian and other buildings in the city were brought together and put on display in the new building. At the same time, the title National Archaeological Museum replaced the earlier identification as the Central Archaeological Museum. And still the collections grew. A decade after the building's completion all the objects belonging to the Archaeological Society were given to the museum, drawing with them contributions from other collections still displayed privately. Expansion of the new museum building was at once necessary, and begun under the direction of another German architect, the Dresdener Ernst Ziller who spent his career in Athens designing many of the capital's fine late nineteenth-century buildings.

Before long the continual addition to the museum collections through archaeological discoveries led to the need for still more galleries. Plans were made and construction begun in 1931. Eight years later the new wing was completed, that section which today houses the bronze collection on the ground floor and the vase collection on the upper. But the year was 1939, an ominous date. Politicians were still speaking of peace, but museum directors throughout Europe were looking for places to store and protect their precious possessions from the approaching storm. When the war tide surged across Greek borders in 1940, all of the objects of the National Museum were removed and buried for protection.

Though the war in Europe was over in 1945, civil war continued in Greece for several more years. However, once Athens itself was free of any fighting, the museum staff began excavating for antiquities, but this time in the very cellars of the museum building where the statues and other art objects had been buried in sand. Even as the civil war still tore at villages in the mountains of Greece, a temporary exhibition of museum objects was placed on display in the new wing which had been completed just prior to the war. At the same time, preparation of the vase collection display was underway on the floor above.

War and time had taken their toll on the older wing of the museum, so it was decided that its galleries should undergo renovation. Even as visitors viewed the treasures temporarily on exhibit in the new wing, the older one was being repaired. Then one by one—beginning with the Mycenaean collection in the central rooms of the ground floor—the galleries were opened, until today the greater part of the collections of the National Archaeological Museum are on display, the largest and most complete exhibition of Greek art to be found anywhere.

The postwar work on the museum galleries gives the nineteenth-century building the clean, bright, uncluttered appearance of the best of modern museums, with beneficent Attic sunlight setting off the art on display most days of the year without need for artificial illumination. Because in most galleries the windows are located high up on the walls, museum visitors do not suffer the reflections and glare surrounding the works of art in other museums. The building's physical features have made both museum work and museum visiting comfortable for staff and public alike.

The collections are displayed in their separate areas of the museum building, most of them arranged in chronological order. This allows one to visit the sculpture collection passing from seventh-century Archaic statues through to first-century B.C. late Hellenistic works. The same time passage is repeated when viewing the vase collection. Exceptions to this chronological arrangement are the Mycenaean and bronze collections, where objects are displayed according to where they were found. There are cases devoted to the finds at Tiryns, at Pylos, Attica and so on. The many finds from Mycenae itself are grouped together according to the site where they were discovered, cases of objects given to the various shaft graves, grave circles and tombs as well as the acropolis of Mycenae. The bronzes are similarly grouped according to site.

Such arrangements of the museum's possessions give an overall view of ancient Greek art in a brief visit, while allowing for a more studied view for those with more time to spend in this very important museum of ancient art.

Most of the collections of the National Museum are anchored to important archaeological finds and the stories of those finds constitute the history of the collections. Though it has been the initial discoveries which have excited the greatest public interest, later finds are often equally important. For example, excellent frescoes were found in a house in the wall of Mycenae in 1970, almost a century after Schliemann began his famous work on that site. The following accounts can only briefly honor those dedicated archaeologists who have made the collections of the National Museum possible.

PREHISTORIC COLLECTIONS
Schliemann's discoveries at Mycenae and later at Tiryns, which began in 1874, serve as the core of the prehistoric collections. As has been noted, excavations at Mycenae have continued ever since with major finds still being made a century later. The objects of other Mycenaean period sites, Carl Blegen's discovery of Pylos in 1939 being a notable example, have contributed greatly to the collection.

Explorations by Christos Tsountas in Thessaly pushed Greek prehistory back to the seventh millennium while bringing to light objects of Neolithic art for the prehistoric collections. Subsequent discoveries of more sites in other areas of Greece have enlarged this part of the prehistoric collections. It was this same Christos Tsountas whose organized excavations in the Cycladic Islands turned up the greater part of the objects displayed in the Cycladic-period collection.

Until recently the museum had no representative examples of Minoan art. However, excavations begun in 1967 by Professor Marinatos on Thera revealed marvelous frescoes of the sixteenth century B.C. when Minoan influence was at its height in the Aegean. Now displayed in the National Museum, they not only give the museum acknowledged Minoan masterworks but serve as evidence of a broader range of subjects rendered by Minoan period artists than had been realized until now.

SCULPTURE COLLECTION
The museum's large collection of sculpture comes from many sites throughout Greece, but some important finds can be mentioned. German and Greek excavations began in 1863 on the Kerameikos, the ancient potters' quarter and main cemetery of ancient Athens. Around the many grave reliefs found there has grown the museum's collection of funerary sculpture. Excavations on the temple and sanctuary of Asklepios at Epidauros, begun in 1882 by Panayiotis Kavvadias, provided the fine pieces of the Epidauros room. Excavations begun in Lykosoura in Arcadia in 1889 and at Rhamnous in Attica a year later supplied the museum with objects from provincial sites, mainly cult statues.

Underwater archaeology and some fisherman's luck has shared in the gathering of important large bronzes with discoveries beneath the sea of Antikythera in 1900, in the Bay of Marathon in 1926 and off Artemision in 1926 and 1928. This has made the museum's collection of large bronzes unique among the world's Classical sculpture collections.

There is no term for understreet archaeology, yet it was street repairs in Piraeus in 1959 which turned up a number of large bronze statues, including the oldest large-scale bronze Greek statue ever found, an Archaic-period Apollo. Few museums can claim as major contributors to their collections ordinary street workers.

BRONZE COLLECTION
Most of the bronzes in the museum collection are small in size and exhibited apart from the larger bronze statues. They too come from a variety of sources, but a few can be mentioned. In 1959, the same year when the large Piraeus bronzes were found, workers digging a ditch for new water pipes in the Ambelokipi section of Athens unearthed a number of bronze statuettes, now in the museum collection.

But bronzes were part of the museum collections from a very early date. From the sacred site of Zeus at Dodona in Epeiros come many examples excavated by Konstantinos Karapanos in the last century. During an untended period, thieves looted the excavation site and smuggled out of the country objects which eventually ended up in the Berlin museum. However a significant amount are owned by the National Museum and exhibited as the Karapanos collection.

Excavations on the Athens Acropolis have contributed to the bronze collection, as have those at Olympia and other sites of ancient religious sanctuaries in the Peloponnesos. They include votive offerings, religious utensils, weapons, and armor, each deserving a studied examination regardless of their small size.

HELEN STATHATOS COLLECTION
The gift of ancient jewellery and other objects from a variety of periods, assembled by Helen Stathatos, is the one example, in the usual sense of the term, of a whole collection given to the museum. Exhibited as a unit, it is the result of a single person's devotion to a lifetime of collecting objects of ancient art with the intent of eventually offering them for public display.

VASE COLLECTION
The upper floor of the museum's new wing offers the large vase collection, with its examples of the Greek potter and painters' art, from the early Geometric period to its waning in the late Classical period. The collection is particularly strong in earlier vases as well as white lekythoi from the Classical period, but includes fine examples from every period. The examples have come from a number of sites, but three in particular should be mentioned as making a substantial contribution to the museum's collection and our knowledge of Greek vase painting.

There is first of all the Kerameikos in Athens and other ancient cemeteries of Attica. From these sites come the many funerary vases which make up a large part of the collection of Geometric period vases. They were also the sources of the white lekythoi which make the National Museum collection of this vase type the largest anywhere.

The cemetery at Vari in Attica has been a rich source of early black-figure vases, especially helpful in identifying the personality of one of the black-figure pioneers, the Nessos Painter, even though his name vase, in the National Museum, was found elsewhere.

Athenian vase painters and potters dedicated vases and plaques on tbe Acropolis. Most were broken and some even charred black when the Persians burned the Acropolis in 480 B.C., so they survive only as broken fragments. Yet, these vase shards have become a remarkable part of the National Museum's vase collection, as they offer several insights not available in most vase collections. In particular, as offerings on the Acropolis, they must have been considered by each artist a major piece of work, not an everyday vase made for the trade, and a close examination of the fragments proves this to have been the case. In their broken state the fragments isolate the painter's art from the vase so that one can better view his style and talent. In addition, several of the fragments have the name of the painter inscribed on them, thereby identifying certain painters, known otherwise only by style without any personal identification.

NUMISMATIC COLLECTION
From the seventh century on, Greek city-states minted coins, changing styles frequently so that they display the stylistic changes apparent in the other arts of sculpture and vase painting. Most excavation sites yield coins, which are often of the greatest aid in dating the site. From such finds the most excellent of examples have been gathered in the National Museum's Greek coin collection, one of the finest to be found anywhere.

PLAN OF THE BUILDING

GROUND FLOOR

1. Entrance
2. North Portico
2A. Casts and reproductions
3. Atrium
4. Mycenaean art
5. Neolithic and pre-Mycenaean art
6. Cycladic art
7-13. Art of the Archaic period
14. Art of the late Archaic period
15. Poseidon Gallery
16-20. Art of the Classical period
21. Diadoumenos Gallery
22. Sculpture from the Sanctuary of
    Asclepios of Epidauros
23-24. Fourth-century funerary steles
25-27. Fourth-century votive and
    commemorative steles
28. Fourth-century funerary steles;
    Youth from Antikythera
29. Themis Gallery
30. Art of the Hellenistic period
31. Temporary exhibitions
32. Stathatos Collection
34. Votive sculpture
35. Stairs to upper floor
36. Karapanos Collection
37. Collection of bronzes
40. Collection of bronzes
41-43. Roman art
Galleries 33, 38, 39, 44, 45, 46. 47
    are closed to the public.

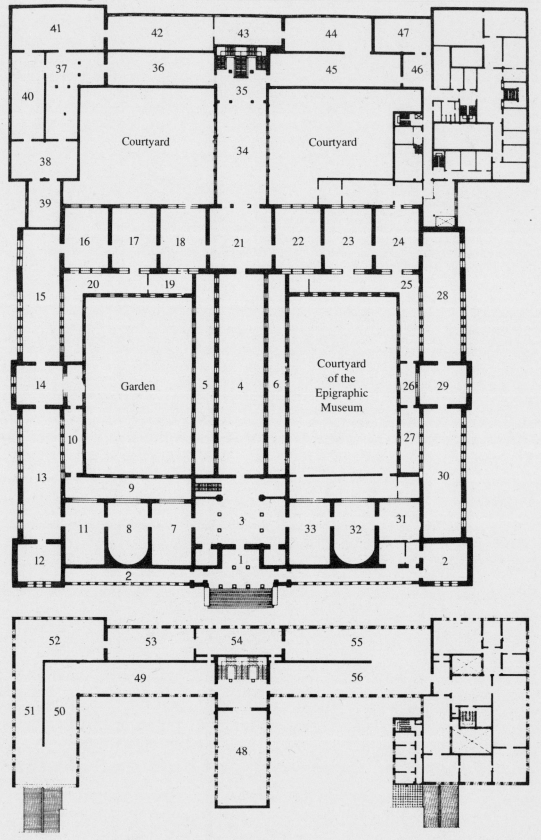

SECOND FLOOR

48. Frescoes from Thera
49-50. Vases of the Geometric period
51. Vases from the cemetery at Vari
52. Sophilos and Heraion of Argos Gallery
53. Black-figure vases
54. Red-figure and black-figure vases
55. White lekythoi and red-figure vases
56. Gallery of the Epinetron of Eretria and
    fourth-century vases

MAP OF ANCIENT GREECE

from Philip's *Atlas of Classical, Historical and Scriptural Geography*, Liverpool, 1855

SELECTED BIBLIOGRAPHY

ATHENS ARCHEOLOGICAL MUSEUM

AMANDRY, P.: *Collection Hélène Stathatos. Les bijoux antiques.* Strasbourg. 1953.

ANDRONICOS, M., CHATZIDAKIS, M., and KARAGEORGHIS, V.: *The Greek Museums.* Athens and New Rochelle, N. Y. 1974.

ANDRONICOS, MANOLIS: *National Museum.* Athens. 1975.

KAROUZOU, S: *Catalogue of the Collection of Sculpture of the National Archeological Museum.* Athens. 1968.

KYPREOU, L.: *National Archeological Museum of Athens.* Athens. 1971.

SAKELLARIOU, A. and PAPATHANASOUPOLOS, G.: *Musée Archéologique National. Collections Préhistoriques. Un guide sommaire.* Athènes. 1965.

STAIS, V.: *Marbres et bronzes du Musée National.* Athènes. 1910.

GENERAL WORKS

CHAMOUX, FRANCOIS: *Greek Art.* Greenwich, Conn., New York Graphic Society. 1966.

CHARBONNEAU, J., MARTIN, R., and VILLARD, F.: *Grèce archaique.* Paris, 1968.

——————: *Grèce classique.* Paris. 1969.

DEMARGNE, PIERRE: *The Birth of Greek Art.* New York. Golden Press. 1964.

RICHTER, G. M. A.: *A Handbook of Greek Art.* London, Phaidon. Revised Edition. 1965.

WEGNER, MAX: *Greek Masterpieces of Art.* New York. Braziller. 1960.

HAFNER, GERMAN: *Art of Crete, Mycenae and Greece.* New York. Abrams. 1968.

PREHISTORIC ART

BLEGEN, C.: *The Mycenaean Age.* Cincinnati. 1952.

EVANS, A.: *The Palace of Minos* (vol. 1–IV). London. 1921–1936.

HIGGINS, REYNOLDS: *Minoan and Mycenaean Art.* New York, Praeger. 1967.

KENNA, V.: *Cretan Seals.* Oxford. 1960.

MARINATOS, S., and HIRMER, M.: *Crete and Mycenae.* New York. Abrams. 1960.

MATZ, FRIEDRICH: *Crete and Early Greece.* New York, Crown. 1962.

MYLONAS, G.: *Mycenae and the Mycenaean Age.* Princeton. 1960.

SCULPTURE

ASHMOLE, B.: *The Classical Ideal in Greek Sculpture.* Cincinnati. 1964.

BIEBER, MARGARETE: *The Sculpture of the Hellenistic Age.* New York. 1961.

HIRMER, M.: *Greek Sculpture.* London. 1960.

JOHANSEN, K. E.: *The Attic Grave-Reliefs of the Classical Period.* Copenhagen. 1951.

RICHTER, G. M. A.: *Kouroi; A Study of the Development of the Kouros Type in Greek Sculpture.* London. 1960.

VASE PAINTING

ARIAS, P. E., and HIRMER, M.: *A History of Greek Vase Painting.* London. 1962.

BEAZLEY, J. D.: *Potter and Painter in Ancient Athens.* London. 1949.

COOK, R. M.: *Greek Painted Pottery.* London. 1960.

DESBOROUGH, V. R. d'A.: *Protogeometric Pottery.* Oxford. 1952.

PHILIPPAKI, BARBARA: *The Attic Stamnos.* Oxford. 1967.

RICHTER, G. M. A.: *Attic Red-Figured Vases.* New Haven. 1958.

WEBSTER, T. B. L.: *Potter and Patron in Classical Athens.* London. 1972.

MINOR ARTS

FRANCKE, P. R. and HIRMER, M.: *Greek Coins as Art.* London, Thames & Hudson. 1965.

HIGGINS, R.: *Greek and Roman Jewellery.* London. 1961.

JENKINS, G. K. *Monnaies Grecques.* Fribourg. 1972.

LAMB, W.: *Greek and Roman Bronzes.* London. 1929.

SELTMAN, C.: *Greek Coins.* London. 1965.

INDEX OF ILLUSTRATIONS

Note: Numbers in italics refer to names in the captions

GENERAL INDEX